THE ULTIMATE AI FOR BEGINNERS GUIDE

A STRESS-FREE GUIDE ON HOW ANYONE CAN LEVERAGE GENERATIVE AI FOR FAST CONTENT CREATION, CAREER SUCCESS, PERSONAL GROWTH, AND INCREASED REVENUE

KEN KIMBERLY

TABLE OF CONTENTS

INTRODUCTION

You wake up, and your digital assistant has already brewed your coffee. Your car suggests the fastest route to the office, dodging traffic jams with ease. You scroll through your phone, and content curated by AI greets you with uncanny accuracy. Welcome to the age of artificial intelligence, a world where technology doesn't just assist but anticipates.

AI is no longer a distant dream of sci-fi enthusiasts; it's embedded in our daily lives. It holds the potential to transform careers, boost creativity, and open up streams of income. Yet, for many, AI remains a mysterious, complex beast. This book is here to change that. It's your guide to understanding and using AI tools like ChatGPT, Dall-e, and others to your advantage. Our aim is to demystify AI and make it accessible to everyone, regardless of background or experience.

This book is designed for those who are curious and eager to learn. Whether you're a young entrepreneur, a seasoned manager, a designer seeking fresh inspiration, or a social media influencer looking for an edge, you'll find value here. If you're new to AI and have questions like, "How can I use this in my daily life?" or "Can AI help me make money?"—you're in the right place. We'll address your concerns and offer practical solutions tailored to your needs.

In the pages ahead, you'll find a roadmap to AI literacy. We start with the basics, making sure you understand the fundamental concepts. Then, we move into practical applications, showing you how to integrate AI into your work and life. We'll explore the nuances of prompt engineering, which is the secret sauce to getting the best out of AI tools. You'll also discover monetization strategies—ways to turn AI into a revenue-generating partner. Ethical considerations follow because with great power comes great responsibility. Finally, we'll peek into the future to see where AI is headed.

What sets this book apart from others is its hands-on approach. We include step-by-step guides that walk you through tasks. There are exercises designed to reinforce learning and real-world examples that show AI in action. You'll read success stories of individuals who have transformed their careers and lives with AI. These elements make the content not just informative but also engaging and practical.

By the end of this book, you'll have a toolkit of skills and knowledge. You'll know how to use AI tools with confidence and create effective prompts that get results. You'll be able to spot opportunities for monetization and understand the ethical landscape of AI. More importantly, you'll have the mindset to continue exploring AI's vast potential.

As you start this journey, keep an open mind. AI is a playground of possibilities waiting to be explored. Be curious, be daring, and don't be afraid to experiment. The only limit is your imagination. So, let's dive in and see what AI can do for you. Welcome to your AI adventure.

CHAPTER 1

UNDERSTANDING AI FUNDAMENTALS

You know that feeling when you walk into a party, and everyone else seems to know what they're doing, leaving you wondering if you missed the memo. That's how many feel about AI. It's the life of the technological party, and yet, it can seem like it's speaking a language all its own. But here's the kicker: AI is actually here to make your life easier, not to confuse you. It's like your best friend who shows up with a map when you're lost. With AI, you can solve problems, enhance creativity, and even make decisions with finesse. But don't worry if it still sounds like techno-babble. We're going to break it down so you can impress at that next shindig—or just use it to make your day-to-day a bit smoother.

1.1 DEMYSTIFYING ARTIFICIAL INTELLIGENCE

Artificial Intelligence, or AI, is a term that gets thrown around a lot, often wrapped in layers of mystique and Hollywood drama. In reality, AI is a tool—one that's incredibly sophisticated but a tool nonetheless. Think of it as a digital assistant that's great at recognizing patterns and solving problems, much like how you would use a calculator to do complex math without breaking a sweat. It doesn't replace human creativity or judgment; instead, it boosts them. Need to sort through heaps of data? AI can do that. Want to brainstorm new ideas? AI's got your back with suggestions that might just spark your next big project. In essence, AI is like the ultimate sidekick, always ready to lend a hand without overshadowing the hero—you.

Now, let's tackle some myths. There's this persistent fear that AI will take over the world, Terminator-style. But let's be real: AI doesn't have dreams of world domination. It lacks autonomy, meaning it can't make decisions without human input. It's designed to complement, not conquer. Consider it a partner that excels at repetitive tasks, freeing you up to focus on what truly requires a human touch. Sure, it can handle mundane chores like a pro, but it still needs you to guide it, making it more of a collaborative teammate than a rogue robot.

Look around, and you'll see AI quietly enhancing your everyday life. It's the voice in your phone, the one that helps you find the nearest coffee shop or reminds you of your appointments—thank you, Siri and Google Assistant. It's also behind those eerily accurate movie recommendations on Netflix and the music playlists on Spotify that seem to know your mood better than you do. Even customer service has gotten a boost with AI chatbots that handle queries faster than you can say "representative." These applications make AI tangible, integrating seamlessly into tasks we often take for granted.

However, it's crucial to understand what AI can and cannot do. AI excels at specific tasks—think of it as a specialized tool rather than a Swiss army knife. It can analyze data at lightning speed but doesn't possess the general intelligence or emotional nuance of a human. This is where human oversight remains vital. AI can process information, but it doesn't understand it the way you do. Its decisions are based on data, not intuition or ethics. So, while AI can suggest the best route to your destination, it still needs you to decide if the scenic route or the faster one is more your style.

AI is a game-changer, not a game-ender. With the proper understanding and application, it can be a powerful ally in both work and play. So, as we continue to unravel the potential of AI, remember that it's here to augment your abilities, not overshadow them. It's about making the complex simple, the mundane manageable, and the impossible possible—one algorithm at a time.

1.2 THE EVOLUTION OF AI: FROM CONCEPT TO REALITY

Artificial intelligence, as a concept, has been around for longer than most people realize. Imagine it's the mid-20th century, and the world is buzzing not just with rock 'n' roll but also with the idea that machines could one day think. Fast forward to 1956, when the term "artificial intelligence" was coined during a conference at Dartmouth College. This was the moment when AI stepped out of science fiction and into the realm of academic curiosity. John McCarthy, Marvin Minsky, and their colleagues launched AI as a field of study, setting the stage for decades of innovation. Along the way, critical figures like Alan Turing, who proposed a test to measure a machine's ability to exhibit intelligent behavior, laid foundational concepts that continue to influence AI research today.

The journey from theory to tangible technology is marked by significant breakthroughs. One of the earliest was the development of neural networks, which mimic the way the human brain processes information. This was a game-changer, allowing machines to learn from data and improve over time. The advent of machine learning and its more sophisticated cousin, deep learning, propelled AI to new heights. These technologies underpin many of the AI tools we use today, enabling computers to recognize speech, translate languages, and even beat humans at complex games like chess and Go. The progress in AI has been nothing short of remarkable, transforming it from an academic curiosity to a powerful force in both technological and cultural landscapes.

As AI evolved, so did its underlying technologies. Initially, AI systems were rule-based, operating under strict logical frameworks that required explicit instructions for every possible scenario. This approach was limiting and often clunky. Over time, a significant shift occurred towards learning-based models. Machine learning emerged, allowing systems to learn from data patterns rather than relying solely on pre-programmed rules. This evolution was fueled by the explosion of big data—vast amounts of information generated by the digital age. With more data and more processing power, AI could move beyond static responses and adapt to new information, making it more versatile and applicable to real-world problems.

Looking ahead, the future of AI is filled with even more possibilities. Quantum computing is on the horizon, promising to exponentially increase computing power and, in turn, AI capabilities. Imagine AI systems that can solve problems in seconds that would take today's fastest supercomputers years to crack. In healthcare, AI could revolutionize diagnostics and personalized medicine, offering treatments tailored to individual genetic profiles. While these developments are still emerging, they signal a future where AI could redefine what's possible in various fields, from transportation to finance.

The story of AI is ongoing, with each chapter more exciting than the last. From its inception in academic halls to its integration into daily life, AI's evolution is a testament to human ingenuity and the relentless pursuit of progress. As we explore further in this book, understanding where AI came from helps illuminate where it might go next.

1.3 EXPLORING CHATGPT: CONVERSATIONAL AI UNPACKED

Let's talk about ChatGPT, a conversational AI so sophisticated it might just be your next best pen pal. At its core, ChatGPT operates on the architecture of Generative Pre-trained Transformers, or GPT for short. Imagine GPT as a brain with layers, each one fine-tuned to understand human language in all its quirky, nuanced glory. It's trained on vast datasets, enabling it to predict and generate text that feels authentically human. This AI doesn't just spit out words; it crafts sentences with a coherence that's as close to human dialogue as we've seen. The magic happens in the layers of the transformer—think of them as neurons in a brain, passing information back and forth until the most logical response emerges. This process allows ChatGPT to engage in conversations on topics as mundane as the weather or as complex as quantum physics, making it incredibly versatile.

ChatGPT's utility stretches far and wide, offering solutions across various fields. In customer service, for instance, it can handle volumes of inquiries with a politeness that never tires, automating responses and freeing human agents for more complicated issues. Content creators find it invaluable; whether drafting articles, editing text, or even brainstorming ideas, ChatGPT provides a creative boost. It acts as a personal virtual assistant, managing tasks like setting reminders or even generating emails, making it an indispensable tool in both professional and personal contexts.

Its capabilities extend to crafting social media posts, writing code snippets, and even composing music. The versatility of ChatGPT means that whether you're a business owner, a writer, or just someone who enjoys a good chat, there's something it can do for you.

Of course, working with ChatGPT isn't without its challenges. One common issue is handling ambiguous questions or instructions. The AI relies heavily on clarity; vague prompts can lead to generic or off-base responses. This means users must learn to be precise in their communication, a skill that can take some practice to perfect. Another challenge is managing expectations. While ChatGPT can generate human-like text, it's not infallible. It can still "hallucinate" or provide convincingly wrong information, especially if the input is unclear or the topic is outside its training data. This requires users to fact-check its outputs and use them as a starting point rather than a final answer.

This brings us to the concept of prompt engineering—a technique as crucial to working with ChatGPT as knowing how to turn on a computer before using one. Crafting effective prompts involves understanding how the AI interprets language and using that to guide it toward desired outcomes. For example, if you want ChatGPT to write a blog post, you might start with a detailed prompt: "Write a 500-word blog post about the benefits of urban gardening, focusing on sustainability and local food production." The specificity helps the AI hone in on the task, reducing the chances of straying off-topic. Successful prompt strategies often involve breaking down complex requests into simple, clear instructions, which can significantly enhance the quality of the AI's output.

Interactive Element: Prompt Crafting Exercise

To get a feel for prompt engineering, try this exercise: Write three different prompts for the task "Generate a recipe." Start with a vague prompt, then refine it for clarity and detail. Observe how each version changes the AI's response. This practice will help you see the impact of prompt specificity on the AI's performance.

1.4 DALL-E AND CREATIVE AI: TRANSFORMING ART AND DESIGN

In the realm of creative AI, Dall-e stands out not just as a tool but as a magician in the digital world. Imagine typing out a description of a two-headed flamingo sipping coffee at a Parisian café, and voilà, Dall-e conjures an image as if sketched by an enigmatic artist. This is the marvel of text-to-image generation, where words become vivid visuals, thanks to the magic of deep learning. Deep learning, the backbone of Dall-e, mimics the human brain, processing and interpreting data to create something entirely new. This isn't just about replication; it's about creation. With each textual input, Dall-e sifts through vast amounts of data, learning and predicting how to translate words into pixels, crafting images that can stir the imagination or illuminate an idea.

The creative possibilities with Dall-e are as boundless as your imagination. In the world of art and illustration, it can generate original pieces that might take a human artist days or even weeks to conceptualize. Dall-e can become an artist's muse, sparking new directions in style or content. Designers, too, find a friend in this AI, using it to prototype concepts and experiment with visual aesthetics without the painstaking detail of manual sketching. Imagine a fashion designer testing out a new line of eco-friendly apparel, visualized in minutes rather than months. In marketing and advertising, Dall-e provides a creative edge, crafting compelling visuals that capture attention and convey messages with clarity and creativity. The ability to rapidly generate and iterate visuals allows marketers to tailor campaigns with a degree of precision and personalization previously unimaginable.

Yet, like any powerful tool, Dall-e comes with its quirks and questions. One of the pressing issues is originality—where does inspiration end and imitation begin? While Dall-e's creations are unique, they are rooted in the data it learns from, which raises questions about copyright and creative ownership. Can an AI-generated image be truly original if it draws from existing works? This leads us to ethical considerations, particularly in media and content. Misuse of AI-generated content can lead to misinformation or deceptive practices. As creators, it is our responsibility to use these tools ethically, ensuring transparency and authenticity in our work.

Looking to the future, the implications of Dall-e and creative AI are profound. We stand on the brink of a new era in art and design where AI could democratize creativity. Imagine a world where anyone, regardless of skill level, can bring their visual ideas to life, fostering a culture where creativity is not limited by technical ability but only by imagination. Collaborative projects may flourish, where humans and AI work in tandem, each enhancing the other's strengths. This partnership could redefine artistic boundaries, leading to creations that neither could achieve alone.

As we explore the potential of Dall-e, it's clear that we're witnessing more than just a technological advancement; it's a cultural shift. AI is reshaping how we create, pushing us to rethink notions of authorship and creativity. By embracing these tools responsibly, we can open doors to innovation that enriches both our personal and professional lives. As we continue to explore the potential of AI, we open ourselves to endless possibilities where imagination and technology walk hand in hand.

Interactive Element: Prompt Crafting Exercise For Image Creation

As in the previous exercise in Prompt Crafting, start with a vague prompt, then refine it for clarity and detail. Go to any AI image creator of your choice and ask it to create an image of a tomato. Then, refine it by asking it to create a line art image of a tomato, then a photorealistic image, etc... Notice how simply adding specificity helps you receive the desired output?

CHAPTER 2

DIVING INTO AI APPLICATIONS

I magine your business operations as a chaotic orchestra, each instrument playing its own tune, oblivious to the conductor. Now, picture AI is stepping onto the podium, baton in hand, transforming that cacophony into a harmonious symphony. That's the power of AI in streamlining business operations. It's not about replacing human ingenuity but enhancing it, creating an environment where efficiency and innovation can dance together.

AI has become the virtuoso of operational efficiency, capable of optimizing even the most mundane tasks. Think of AI-driven inventory management systems as your backstage crew, ensuring everything is in its place before the curtain rises. These systems can track stock levels with precision, automatically reorder when supplies run low, and predict future needs based on trends. It's like having a crystal ball but without the need for a mystical tent or a dubious fortune teller. With predictive analytics, AI can forecast demand, allowing businesses to prepare for the future rather than merely react to it. This foresight reduces waste, cuts costs, and ensures that you're always ahead of the curve, ready to meet customer needs before they even know they have them.

Customer relationship management (CRM) is another area where AI shines brighter than a spotlight on opening night. Imagine a world where every customer interaction feels personalized, like a tailored suit or a bespoke piece of jewelry. AI makes this possible by analyzing customer data to predict preferences and personalize interactions. Automated chatbots handle inquiries with the charm of a seasoned concierge, providing swift, accurate responses and reducing the burden on human staff. Meanwhile, personalization algorithms work behind the scenes, customizing marketing strategies to suit individual tastes and preferences. It's marketing magic, turning data into delightful customer experiences.

Then there's the supply chain, the unsung hero of any business, quietly working away to get products from A to B. AI steps in here like a skilled logistics manager, optimizing routes, reducing costs, and improving delivery times. It can analyze traffic patterns, weather forecasts, and historical data to ensure deliveries are as efficient as a Swiss watch. Real-time tracking means you're never in the dark about where your shipments are, providing peace of mind and the ability to tackle potential issues before they escalate. It's like having a GPS for your entire supply chain, ensuring everything runs smoothly and on time.

Human resources might seem like an unlikely candidate for AI's touch, but it's proving to be a game-changer in recruitment and employee engagement. AI-driven talent acquisition platforms sift through resumes faster than you can say "you're hired," identifying the best candidates with an accuracy that rivals a seasoned recruiter. By analyzing vast amounts of data, these platforms can predict candidate success and fit, making the hiring process more efficient and effective. But AI doesn't stop at hiring. It also helps keep employees engaged by analyzing feedback with sentiment analysis and identifying trends and areas for improvement. It's like having a trusted advisor who listens to every concern and offers solutions that keep your workforce happy and productive.

Interactive Element: Self-Assessment for AI Integration

Take a moment to reflect on your current business operations. Consider the following questions: Are there areas where AI could enhance efficiency? Could AI-driven tools improve customer interactions or streamline your supply chain? Use these prompts to identify potential opportunities for AI integration in your business. This exercise will help you envision how AI can transform your operations and set the stage for implementation.

In essence, AI is the ultimate multitasker, capable of handling various aspects of business operations with ease and precision. It's not just about making things faster or cheaper; it's about creating more intelligent, more responsive systems that adapt to changing needs and help businesses thrive in an ever-evolving landscape. Whether you're an entrepreneur looking to scale your startup, a manager seeking operational improvements, or someone new to AI eager to understand its potential, this chapter offers insights into how AI can become an indispensable ally in your business endeavors.

2.1 ENHANCING CREATIVITY WITH AI TOOLS

Imagine your creativity as a painter with an endless palette of colors; only now, AI hands you a brush that can paint your ideas into existence faster and with more flair. AI isn't here to steal the show but to serve as a creative partner, adding depth and dimension to your artistic endeavors. When brainstorming feels as if you're chasing ideas in a fog, AI steps in like a lighthouse, illuminating pathways you might not have seen. It generates and refines concepts, offering fresh angles and insights. AI-assisted brainstorming isn't just about speed; it's about enhancing your creative process, ensuring no good idea is left unexplored. Picture AI as your creative muse, suggesting new themes, styles, or even entire plotlines for your next novel or marketing campaign.

In the realm of content creation, AI is like having a multi-talented artist at your fingertips. Whether you need music, video, or prose, AI can assist you in crafting content that resonates. Let's say you're a budding songwriter who hums tunes but struggles with lyrics. AI can help you generate lines that fit your melody, offering suggestions that inspire and refine your work. For video production, imagine an AI that can edit footage with the precision of a seasoned director, cutting and splicing to create seamless transitions and captivating narratives. This isn't about letting AI take over but about letting it handle the grunt work so you can focus on the creative vision. It's an ally in your mission to produce captivating content, whether you're crafting a viral video or composing a symphony.

Design and architecture are fields where visual imagination reigns supreme, and AI is stepping up as a powerful collaborator. In architecture, AI tools can assist in generative design, where algorithms explore countless design permutations based on specified criteria. This opens up a world where architects can push the boundaries of what's possible, experimenting with forms and structures that may have been too complex or time-consuming to realize manually. In design, AI aids in 3D modeling and rendering, turning concepts into detailed visualizations swiftly. It allows designers to iterate and test ideas without committing to costly prototypes, making the creative process more efficient and flexible. Whether it's a skyscraper or a piece of furniture, AI ensures your designs are both innovative and practical, marrying creativity with functionality.

Collaborative projects between AI tools and human creators are not science fiction; they're happening now, and they're producing stunning results. Take art projects that blend human intuition with AI's analytical prowess. Artists can feed AI their sketches or concepts and, in return, receive variations that challenge their perspectives and push their creativity beyond traditional boundaries. In film, AI-assisted scriptwriting is transforming storytelling. Writers use AI to develop plotlines, characters, and dialogue, creating richer narratives by exploring possibilities they might not have considered. It's a dance of creativity where AI complements human imagination, allowing creators to experiment and innovate with a safety net of suggestions and insights. This symbiosis of man and machine doesn't dilute creativity; it enriches it, offering new dimensions and possibilities in artistic expression.

Imagine AI as a backstage assistant for your creative process, always ready with a suggestion or a helping hand. It doesn't replace the thrill of creation but amplifies it, providing tools that are as versatile as they are innovative. Whether you're composing music, designing skyscrapers, or writing the next blockbuster screenplay, AI is there to elevate your work, turning creative challenges into opportunities for brilliance. It's a partnership where your imagination sets the stage, and AI helps bring the vision to life, ensuring the spotlight shines just a little brighter on your creative endeavors.

2.2 AI-DRIVEN SOCIAL MEDIA STRATEGIES

Navigating the world of social media can feel like juggling flaming torches while riding a unicycle—thrilling but precarious.

Enter AI, your new best friend. AI-powered social media management tools are the backstage crew, ensuring your act goes off without a hitch. Imagine a world where content scheduling, audience engagement, and analytics are all automated, leaving you to focus on creativity and strategy. With AI-based social media analytics tools, you get insights into what works and what doesn't, all while sipping your morning coffee. These tools analyze engagement metrics, sentiment, and reach, offering a clear picture of your social media landscape. Automated post-scheduling and engagement algorithms then take the wheel, ensuring your content reaches your audience at the perfect time. It's like having a 24/7 social media manager who never asks for a day off.

AI doesn't just stop at making life easier; it's about making it smarter. Content personalization and targeting have become the new norm, and AI is the wizard behind the curtain. It sifts through mountains of data to tailor content to specific audiences, making every post feel like it was crafted just for them. Personalized ad targeting ensures your message lands with the right people, maximizing engagement and conversion rates. Meanwhile, dynamic content adaptation adjusts your posts in real time based on user behavior, ensuring relevance and resonance. It's the difference between shouting into the void and having a meaningful conversation with your audience.

Then there's sentiment analysis—AI's way of reading the room. Imagine being able to gauge public sentiment towards your brand at a glance. Sentiment tracking tools do just that, analyzing comments, mentions, and reviews to provide a snapshot of brand reputation. This data informs your strategy, guiding content decisions and highlighting areas for improvement. AI-based feedback loops allow for continuous refinement, ensuring your content remains impactful and engaging. It's like having a focus group that never sleeps, providing real-time insights into audience perceptions.

Influencer marketing is where AI truly shines. Finding the right influencer can be like searching for a needle in a haystack, but AI transforms it into a breeze. AI-driven influencer identification platforms analyze social media trends, engagement metrics, and audience demographics to pinpoint influencers who align with your brand values. This not only optimizes partnerships but also elevates campaign success. Analytics tools then measure influencer impact, tracking campaign metrics to ensure you're getting bang for your buck. It's marketing magic, turning data into dynamic partnerships that drive results.

Interactive Element: Social Media Audit Checklist

Before diving into AI tools, conduct a social media audit. Use this checklist to evaluate your current strategy: Are your posts engaging? Is your audience growing? What content performs best? Identify strengths and areas for improvement to refine your approach. This exercise will help you understand your starting point, setting the stage for AI-driven enhancements.

In the ever-evolving world of social media, AI is not just a tool; it's a game-changer. It automates the mundane, personalizes the experience, and provides insights that drive strategy. Whether you're a social media influencer, a small business owner, or just someone looking to boost your online presence, AI offers the tools to elevate your efforts. It's about working smarter, not harder, ensuring your social media strategy is as dynamic as the platforms themselves.

2.3 REAL-WORLD CASE STUDIES: SUCCESS WITH AI

Think about walking into a store where everything you see feels like it was chosen specifically for you. This isn't a retail utopia; it's AI at work, crafting personalized shopping experiences that leave customers delighted. Retailers have tapped into AI's power to analyze consumer behavior, using data to tailor shopping experiences to individual tastes. Imagine AI as your personal shopper, knowing your preferences, suggesting items you didn't even know you wanted, and optimizing inventory so that your favorite products are always available. This isn't just about making a sale; it's about building loyalty and creating a shopping experience that feels less transactional and more personal.

In healthcare, AI has stepped into the role of a savvy diagnostician, predicting health issues before they become critical. Through predictive diagnostics, AI processes vast datasets of medical histories and genetic information, identifying patterns that might escape even the most experienced human eye. It's like having a doctor who never sleeps, continuously learning and improving. Patients receive more accurate diagnoses and personalized treatment plans, reducing unnecessary tests and procedures. This not only improves patient outcomes but also streamlines operations and reduces costs in the healthcare system, making it a win-win for providers and patients alike.

Lessons from these case studies are valuable for anyone looking to integrate AI into their own ventures. One key takeaway is the importance of aligning AI initiatives with business goals. AI isn't a magic wand; it needs clear objectives to be effective. Businesses must identify specific problems AI can solve and then tailor solutions to meet these needs. It's also crucial to be aware of the potential challenges in AI deployment. From data privacy concerns to integration issues, companies must navigate these hurdles with careful planning and strategy. Those who succeed are often those who take a thoughtful approach, viewing AI as a strategic partner rather than just another tool.

AI's versatility shines in various industries, each with its unique applications. In finance, AI is the vigilant watchdog, detecting fraud and managing risks with greater precision than any human could achieve. It analyzes transaction patterns, flagging anomalies that could indicate fraudulent activity, thus protecting both businesses and consumers. In education, AI creates personalized learning platforms that adapt to each student's pace and style. Imagine an AI tutor who knows exactly when you need a hint or when you're ready for a challenge. This not only boosts student engagement but also improves learning outcomes by tailoring education to individual needs.

The return on investment (ROI) of AI is tangible and compelling. Through process automation, businesses save time and resources, redirecting human effort to more strategic tasks. This not only cuts costs but also enhances efficiency, allowing companies to do more with less. Customer satisfaction sees a noticeable uptick as services become faster and more tailored to individual needs. Take the case of a bank using AI to streamline customer service. With automated systems handling routine inquiries, human agents can focus on complex issues, providing a level of service that builds trust and loyalty. The competitive edge gained through such strategic AI integration is hard to overstate, as companies find themselves better equipped to meet evolving market demands.

As we explore these success stories, it's clear that AI's potential is vast and varied. Whether you're in finance, healthcare, education, or any other sector, the opportunities to leverage AI are boundless. The key is to approach AI strategically, aligning it with your goals and addressing challenges head-on. With thoughtful implementation, AI can transform not just individual businesses but entire industries, creating value and driving innovation at every turn. This is just the beginning of our exploration into AI's capabilities. As we move forward, we'll delve deeper into how AI can be applied in new and exciting ways.

CHAPTER 3
MASTERING AI PROMPTS

You know that moment when you're trying to get your dog to sit, and you realize it's all in the tone of your voice and maybe a little hint of a treat? Welcome to the world of AI prompt engineering, where the right prompt is like that perfect tone—clear, concise, and just the right amount of coaxing. Prompt engineering is the art of crafting instructions for AI models to get them to deliver exactly what you need. It's not magic, but it might feel that way once you see the results. Essentially, it's about communication—telling your AI model what you want in a way it understands, like explaining the rules of chess to a curious kid without losing them in the jargon.

At the heart of AI interaction, prompts serve as the steering wheel guiding the AI through the vast highways of its dataset. Imagine you're the captain of a ship, and your prompt is the map plotting the course. A well-crafted prompt is the difference between a smooth sail and a wayward journey into the Bermuda Triangle of AI responses. These prompts shape how AI models, like ChatGPT or Dall-e, interpret and respond to your requests.

They influence the AI's ability to process your input and produce an output that is not only relevant but also insightful and useful. A poorly constructed prompt is like asking a toddler to explain quantum physics—you might get a response, but it won't be what you're looking for.

Clarity and context are the cornerstones of effective, prompt engineering. Think of it like giving directions to a stranger who's never been to your city—you wouldn't just say, "Go to that coffee shop." Instead, you'd specify, "Walk two blocks north to the corner of Maple Street, where you'll see a red brick building with 'Java Jive' in neon lights." Specific language helps direct the AI, ensuring it doesn't wander off into unrelated territories. Incorporating context is equally crucial. Just as you wouldn't start a story in the middle, providing background helps the AI understand the bigger picture, allowing it to deliver nuanced, context-rich responses. Without context, the AI is like a detective without clues—lost and guessing.

Prompts come in various flavors, each suited to different tasks. Open-ended prompts are like throwing a ball into an open field, allowing the AI to explore and generate creative responses. These are great for brainstorming sessions or when you want the AI to surprise you with its ingenuity. On the other hand, specific prompts are akin to asking for a precise recipe—direct and to the point, ideal for when you need detailed, accurate information. Then, there are sequential prompts that guide the AI through complex tasks in steps, much like following a recipe from start to finish. These are perfect for tasks requiring order and logic, ensuring the AI doesn't skip a step or add too much salt to the soup.

Learning the basic techniques of prompt engineering is akin to mastering the basics of a new language. It starts with keywords and phrases, the building blocks of effective communication. These are your tools for highlighting what's important and steering the AI's focus. Structuring prompts for optimal results is the next step, akin to crafting a compelling argument—clear, logical, and persuasive. A well-structured prompt guides the AI like a well-written script, ensuring the performance is spot-on every time. By mastering these techniques, you not only improve the quality of your AI interactions but also unlock the full potential of these powerful tools, turning them into invaluable allies in your creative and professional endeavors.

Interactive Element: Prompt Engineering Exercise

To hone your prompt engineering skills, try crafting three prompts for the task "Describe a day in the life of a digital nomad." Start with a broad prompt, then refine it for specificity and context. Compare the responses to see how clarity and detail affect AI output. This exercise will help you understand the impact of well-crafted prompts in guiding AI models effectively.

3.1 CRAFTING EFFECTIVE CHATGPT PROMPTS

Picture ChatGPT as your overly eager friend who wants to help but needs clear instructions to do so. This AI's response mechanism is like an artist waiting for a theme to paint. The way you phrase your prompts can dramatically shape the outcome of its responses. A well-crafted prompt is the secret sauce that turns a bland AI interaction into a gourmet experience. Consider prompt phrasing like a chef seasoning a dish; too much or too little can ruin the flavor, but the right balance brings out the best. When crafting prompts, aim for a Goldilocks zone—not too vague, not too detailed, but just right. This balance ensures that

ChatGPT can deliver responses that are both relevant and engaging.

Writing direct prompts is akin to giving ChatGPT a GPS for its responses. Ambiguity is your nemesis here; it turns a straightforward task into a wild goose chase. Instead of saying, "Tell me about the weather," direct prompts are more like, "What's the weather forecast for San Francisco this weekend?" This specificity cuts through confusion, guiding ChatGPT to deliver precise, valuable information. Use questions that are as clear as a bell. Direct questions serve as a compass, pointing ChatGPT precisely where you want it to go. Avoiding ambiguity is like clearing a path through a jungle of possibilities, making sure the AI doesn't wander off into the weeds.

Now, let's talk about adding some zest to your prompts for content that's not just accurate but also engaging. Creative prompting is your toolkit for storytelling and narrative building. Imagine asking ChatGPT to weave a tale from a simple prompt: "Create a story about a time-traveling detective in Victorian London." This kind of prompt invites ChatGPT to stretch its narrative muscles, concocting plots and characters that captivate. Hypothetical scenarios are another playground for creativity, allowing ChatGPT to explore "what if" situations. These prompts open doors to innovative ideas, making it an excellent ally for brainstorming sessions where the sky's the limit.

Let's bring this to life with practical examples. In customer service, a well-structured prompt can transform a generic query into a personalized interaction. Instead of a bland "Help me with my order," try. "I placed an order on March 5th, and it was delayed. Can you check its status?" This specificity helps ChatGPT address the customer's needs efficiently. For content creation, use prompts like "Generate ten blog post ideas about sustainable living for urban dwellers." This not only guides ChatGPT but also sparks creativity, leading to unique content ideas that resonate with your audience. Whether you're crafting a marketing campaign or writing a novel, the right prompts can unlock a treasure trove of creativity.

Reflection Section: Explore Your Prompting Style

Consider your current approach to prompting. Reflect on a recent interaction with ChatGPT and evaluate the clarity and effectiveness of your prompt. How could you modify your phrasing to achieve better results? Write down your thoughts and strategies for improvement, keeping these insights in mind for future interactions. This reflective exercise will enhance your prompting skills, allowing you to communicate more effectively with AI models.

3.2 DESIGNING DALL-E PROMPTS FOR STUNNING VISUALS

Imagine Dall-e as a digital artist waiting for your instructions to paint a masterpiece. The magic lies in how it interprets your prompts to create visual wonders. At its core, Dall-e transforms text into images by analyzing the descriptive cues you provide. Think of it as feeding a painter words instead of paint colors. The more precise and vivid your language, the more striking the result. Descriptive language is the linchpin here; it's the difference between asking for "a tree" and "a towering oak tree with golden leaves rustling in a gentle autumn breeze." This specificity guides Dall-e, enabling it to craft images that align closely with your vision. Striking a balance between creativity and precision is crucial. You want to give Dall-e enough room to explore its creative potential while ensuring it doesn't wander too far off the mark. It's about finding that sweet spot where you direct yet inspire, guiding the AI but also allowing it to surprise you with its interpretation.

The key to writing descriptive prompts is tapping into sensory language. Imagine you're describing a scene to someone who can't see it—what details would you include? Is there a splash of red in a sunset, a hint of lavender in a field, or the gleam of moonlight on a calm sea? By incorporating colors, styles, and emotions, you breathe life into your prompts. Think of it as setting the stage for a play where Dall-e is both actor and director. This approach marries the technical with the artistic, ensuring that the AI doesn't just paint but conveys mood and atmosphere. It's like giving a director a script full of rich, vivid scenes to bring to life. Your words become the brushstrokes, and Dall-e is the canvas that captures them.

Experimentation is where things get really exciting. Prompting Dall-e to combine abstract concepts can lead to unexpected, unique creations. Imagine asking for an image of "nostalgia wrapped in the warmth of a summer afternoon" or "the sound of jazz as a swirling dance of colors." These prompts challenge Dall-e to stretch its creative boundaries, much like a jazz musician improvising on stage. Juxtaposing imagery, like "a skyscraper growing out of a forest," can result in artistic effects that are both thought-provoking and visually stunning. This is where Dall-e shines, using its vast dataset to merge concepts in ways that might not occur to the human mind. It's the perfect playground for those who like to push the envelope of creativity, exploring what happens when the familiar meets the fantastical.

To see these ideas in action, consider the world of marketing visuals. A prompt like "Create an image of a futuristic cityscape at dusk with neon lights reflecting off rain-slicked streets" provides enough detail to guide Dall-e while allowing room for its creative flair. For art projects, try something like "Illustrate a dreamlike garden where flowers bloom in the colors of the rainbow under a lavender sky." These prompts use best practices by balancing specificity with creative freedom, leading to outputs that are both accurate and imaginative. The goal is to leverage Dall-e's strengths, helping it to translate your vision into reality with precision and artistry. Prompts should act like a director's notes, clear yet open to interpretation, to guide the AI in crafting visuals that are both stunning and meaningful.

3.3 TROUBLESHOOTING PROMPT CHALLENGES

Crafting prompts for AI can be a bit like teaching a cat to fetch. It might not always work on the first try, and sometimes you'll get a baffling result. Let's face it, we've all been there—typing out what seems to be a perfectly reasonable prompt, only to be met with an AI response that makes us question our life choices. The most common gremlin in this process? Ambiguity. Ambiguous prompts leave too much room for interpretation, causing the AI to wander off course, much like a squirrel chasing its own tail. Similarly, irrelevant responses often stem from prompts that lack clear direction, leading the AI to grasp at straws. The trick is to guide the AI with precision, much like a maestro conducting an orchestra. If your prompt feels like a riddle even to you, it's time to rethink and rephrase. Dial down the vagueness, zero in on specifics, and watch as your AI partner starts to deliver content that's not just relevant but also insightful.

Refining prompts is an iterative process akin to sculpting a masterpiece out of a block of marble. It's rarely perfect on the first chip, so patience and persistence are your best allies. One effective technique is implementing feedback loops. Think of them as your AI's report card, helping you learn from each interaction to hone your prompts further. After each round of interaction, take note of what worked and what didn't. This insight is invaluable for tweaking prompts to enhance their efficacy. Experiment with different phrases, structures, and levels of detail, testing variations to find the sweet spot that elicits the best results. It's like trying on various outfits before a big date—you'll know when you've found the right fit. By consistently refining your approach, you'll soon master the skill of crafting prompts that are both precise and flexible.

Adaptive prompting techniques come into play when you need to respond to AI's feedback dynamically. Imagine you're a detective piecing together clues from a chatty suspect. Recognizing patterns in AI responses can reveal much about how it processes information, offering clues on how to adjust your prompts. If you notice the AI consistently veering off-topic, it might be time to reevaluate the context or specificity of your prompt. Adaptation is key; modify your approach to better align with the AI's response patterns. This can involve tweaking the prompt's context, rephrasing for clarity, or even breaking down complex tasks into simpler steps. By becoming an adaptive prompter, you're essentially learning to speak the AI's language, enabling more fluid and meaningful interactions.

Let's put these strategies into practice with some examples. Suppose your initial prompt, "Tell me about travel," results in a generic list of destinations. You could revise it to "Describe the cultural highlights of Tokyo for a first-time visitor." This version narrows the focus, guiding the AI towards a more targeted response. For layered prompts, tackling complex subjects like "Explain the process of photosynthesis and its impact on the environment" can overwhelm the AI. Instead, break it down:

"What is photosynthesis?" followed by "How does photosynthesis affect the environment?" This approach allows the AI to address each aspect thoroughly, leading to a richer, more cohesive output. By practicing these techniques, you'll not only troubleshoot issues effectively but also elevate the quality of your AI-generated content.

CHAPTER 4
MONETIZING AI FOR FINANCIAL GROWTH

I magine you've just discovered a treasure chest, but instead of gold coins, it's filled with AI algorithms ready to boost your bank account. AI is not just a tool for tech enthusiasts—it's the golden goose of the digital age, laying opportunities at your feet. From revolutionizing industries to creating wealth from thin air, AI holds the potential to transform financial landscapes with the ease of a magician pulling rabbits out of hats. So, how do you turn this magic into money? Let's open this treasure chest and see what AI-powered wonders await.

The first glimmering gem inside is AI-driven data analysis services. In today's data-saturated world, businesses crave insights like a parched traveler craves water. This is where you come in, offering data analysis as a service. Whether you're helping a retail chain predict buying trends or assisting a healthcare provider in patient outcome analysis, the demand for data-driven insights is astronomical. Companies are willing to pay top dollar for services that transform raw data into actionable intelligence. With AI, you can sift through mountains of information, finding patterns and insights that would take a human team a lifetime to uncover. It's not just about crunching numbers; it's about telling a story with the data, turning chaos into clarity.

Next up, we have custom AI solutions for businesses. Picture AI as the Swiss Army knife of technology—versatile, efficient, and indispensable. Businesses need tailored solutions that address specific challenges, whether it's optimizing supply chains or automating customer service. By offering custom AI solutions, you become the architect of digital transformation, crafting tools that solve unique business problems. This could involve developing AI models that enhance customer engagement or streamline operations, each tailored to the client's needs. The value here is in customization—no two businesses are alike, and AI solutions should reflect that individuality. It's about turning AI's capabilities into a bespoke suit, fitting each business like a glove.

Licensing AI technology is another goldmine waiting to be tapped. If you've developed an AI tool that's the cat's pajamas, why not let others in on the action? By licensing your technology, you allow other businesses to use your innovations, all while earning a steady stream of revenue. It's like lending out a prized possession, but instead of wear and tear, it brings in dividends. This approach not only monetizes your invention but also establishes your brand as a leader in the AI space. Companies are eager to leverage proven AI solutions without reinventing the wheel, providing you with a lucrative opportunity to capitalize on your expertise.

Now, let's talk about AI-as-a-Service (AIaaS) models, the subscription-based Netflix of AI offerings. This model allows businesses to access sophisticated AI tools without developing them from scratch. It's a win-win—companies get AI capabilities with minimal investment while you enjoy recurring revenue. Imagine providing AI analytics platforms on demand, where clients can tap into machine learning insights whenever they need them. The beauty of AIaaS is in its scalability and flexibility, catering to businesses of all sizes. From startups needing basic analytics to giants requiring complex data models, AIaaS offers a buffet of options. It's about democratizing AI, making it accessible and affordable for everyone.

AI's potential doesn't stop there; it extends into product development, creating innovative offerings that meet market demands. AI-enhanced software applications are revolutionizing how we interact with technology, from smart assistants that learn your habits to apps that predict your needs before you express them. In consumer electronics, AI drives innovation, bringing forth gadgets that anticipate user behavior and adapt seamlessly. Imagine fridges that order groceries or thermostats that optimize energy use—AI is at the heart of these innovations. By leveraging AI in product development, you can create offerings that not only meet but exceed consumer expectations, positioning your brand at the cutting edge of technology.

And let's not forget AI's role in automation and efficiency. In a world where time is money, AI-powered solutions streamline operations, reducing costs and boosting profitability. Take supply chain logistics, where AI optimizes routes, reduces fuel consumption, and improves delivery times. It's like having a logistics wizard ensuring everything runs like clockwork. In the realm of finance, automated trading systems harness AI to execute trades with precision and speed, maximizing returns while minimizing risks. These systems analyze market trends in real time, making decisions that outpace human counterparts. By embracing AI for automation, businesses can operate with unprecedented efficiency, turning potential into profit with every transaction.

Interactive Element: AI Monetization Checklist

To kickstart your revenue journey, use this checklist to explore potential AI monetization avenues. Consider: What unique data analysis services can you offer? Are there custom AI solutions you can develop for clients? Could you license existing AI technology? Use this checklist to brainstorm ideas, evaluate opportunities, and identify the best strategies for leveraging AI in your financial growth. This exercise will help focus your efforts, ensuring you capitalize on AI's potential effectively.

4.1 SIDE HUSTLES WITH AI: OPPORTUNITIES TO EXPLORE

Imagine making money while sipping coffee in your pajamas. Sounds like a dream, right? Well, welcome to the world of AI side hustles, where you can turn that dream into reality with minimal investment. One of the most feasible options is AI-driven freelance data analysis. Companies are drowning in data, and they need a lifeguard. That's where you step in, armed with AI tools. You can offer services to analyze and interpret data, helping businesses make smarter decisions. It's like being a detective, but instead of solving crimes, you're uncovering patterns and insights that can drive growth.

Developing AI chatbots for small businesses is another lucrative path. Picture yourself as a tech wizard, conjuring digital assistants that handle customer inquiries with the charm of a seasoned receptionist. Small businesses crave efficiency but often lack the resources for round-the-clock customer service. By creating chatbots, you provide a cost-effective solution that enhances their customer experience. It's a win-win—you earn while they save money and boost their service levels. The beauty of this side hustle? You don't need a degree in rocket science.

With the right tools and a bit of creativity, you can develop chatbots that meet specific business needs.

Niche markets are like hidden treasure maps in the vast AI landscape. By focusing on them, you can carve out a space where competition is low but demand is high. Consider offering AI solutions tailored for local businesses. A bakery might need an AI system to optimize order tracking, while a boutique could use AI to personalize marketing campaigns. These are not cookie-cutter solutions; they require customization and a personal touch. Developing custom AI applications for specific industries, like healthcare or real estate, can also open doors to unique opportunities. It's about identifying gaps and filling them with AI-powered solutions that cater to particular needs.

Freelancing with AI skills is like having a Swiss Army knife in the gig economy. Whether you're offering AI consultancy services or creating AI-generated content for clients, the possibilities are vast. Imagine helping a company automate its processes or advising them on AI integration strategies. Your skills can streamline their operations, saving time and resources. Or, picture yourself as a content creator, using AI to generate articles, graphics, or even music. These skills not only enhance your portfolio but also provide flexibility and extra income. It's the perfect blend of creativity and technology, allowing you to work on your terms.

Balancing a side hustle with your day job can feel like juggling flaming swords while riding a unicycle. But fear not because AI can help you keep those swords in the air. Leverage AI to automate tasks, freeing up time for the things that matter most. Whether it's scheduling social media posts or managing emails, AI tools can handle the mundane so you can focus on growth. Setting realistic goals and timelines is crucial. Think of it as mapping out a road trip—you wouldn't try to drive from New

York to L.A. in a day. Break down your objectives into manageable chunks, and celebrate each milestone along the way. This approach keeps you motivated and prevents burnout, ensuring your side hustle remains a source of joy, not stress.

4.2 SUCCESS STORIES: ENTREPRENEURS WHO THRIVED WITH AI

Once upon a time, in the bustling tech ecosystems of Silicon Valley and beyond, a new breed of entrepreneurs emerged—those who saw AI not as a distant future but as a present opportunity. Take, for example, the founders of an AI-powered startup that began in a small garage (yes, the classic tech origin story). These visionaries identified a gap in the market for personalized customer interactions. They developed an AI-driven platform that transformed how businesses engage with their customers, using natural language processing to create meaningful conversations. What started as a modest operation quickly scaled into a multimillion-dollar enterprise, demonstrating AI's potential to revolutionize traditional customer service models.

But it's not just startups making waves. Innovators in established industries are using AI to push boundaries. Picture an agricultural entrepreneur who harnessed AI to optimize crop yields. By deploying AI sensors and data analytics, they could predict weather patterns and soil conditions with astonishing accuracy. This innovation not only increased productivity but also minimized waste, offering a more sustainable approach to farming. In sectors as diverse as finance, healthcare, and manufacturing, AI is spurring growth and efficiency, allowing businesses to thrive in a competitive landscape. AI doesn't just enhance operations; it redefines them, turning traditional methods on their heads and creating new standards for success.

Career transitions into AI are becoming more common, too. Consider the story of an HR manager who, intrigued by AI's potential, decided to pivot their career. They invested time in learning AI skills and eventually developed an AI-powered recruitment tool that improved hiring processes. With AI, they could analyze candidate data and match skills to job requirements more effectively than ever. This transition not only boosted their career but also highlighted AI's transformative power across different fields. AI isn't just for tech nerds—it's for anyone willing to learn and adapt, showcasing its versatility and accessibility. The stories of these individuals prove that with the right mindset, AI can open doors to new career paths and opportunities.

The key strategies behind these successes are innovation and adaptability. In the fast-paced world of AI, the ability to pivot and embrace new ideas is paramount. Entrepreneurs who thrived with AI often did so by viewing challenges as opportunities. When faced with technological hurdles, they didn't throw in the towel. Instead, they sought creative solutions, whether through collaboration or by leveraging emerging AI technologies. They understood that AI is not a static field; it's a dynamic, evolving landscape that rewards those who are curious and resilient. By staying informed and being willing to take risks, these entrepreneurs carved niches where others saw only obstacles.

AI's impact on business growth is profound. Companies that integrate AI into their operations often see a significant increase in scalability. AI allows for the automation of routine tasks, freeing up human resources to focus on strategic initiatives. This scalability is particularly evident in sectors like e-commerce, where AI-driven recommendation systems enhance customer experiences and increase sales. By predicting customer preferences, businesses can tailor their offerings, creating a competitive edge. This isn't just about keeping up with the competition; it's about setting the pace and redefining what's possible in your industry.

A forward-thinking mindset is crucial for success in AI entrepreneurship. Those who thrive do so by embracing continuous learning and development. They recognize that AI is a field of constant innovation, and staying ahead requires a commitment to expanding one's knowledge base. These entrepreneurs are not afraid to take calculated risks with AI initiatives, knowing that failure is often a stepping stone to success. By fostering a culture of experimentation, they create environments where creativity thrives and new ideas can flourish. This mindset not only drives individual success but also promotes a broader culture of innovation, inspiring others to explore what AI can offer.

4.3 BUILDING A BUSINESS MODEL AROUND AI

Creating a sustainable business model around AI is like piecing together a puzzle, where each piece represents an opportunity or challenge. The first step is identifying your target market and understanding their specific needs. Imagine you're a detective gathering clues about what your potential customers struggle with and what solutions they crave. This involves researching market trends, analyzing competitors, and even talking directly to potential users. Understanding whether your AI offering is a game-changer for tech-savvy entrepreneurs or a lifesaver for small business owners can guide your strategy and ensure you're not just tossing another app into an already crowded sea.

Differentiation is the next piece of the puzzle. In a world where everyone and their grandma seems to be diving into AI, standing out is crucial. This means honing in on what makes your AI solution unique. Perhaps your chatbot can not only answer queries but also whip up a witty joke or two, making customer interactions more engaging. Or maybe your data analysis tool doesn't just churn out numbers but provides actionable insights that even a non-techie can understand. Whatever your edge, make it clear and compelling. Differentiation isn't just about bells and whistles; it's about offering genuine value that sets you apart from the rest, ensuring your solution is the one customers remember.

Now, let's talk about money—specifically, pricing strategies. Pricing AI products and services can feel like walking a tightrope. You want to reflect the value of your offering without scaring off potential customers with sticker shock. This is where value-based pricing models come into play. Instead of basing your price purely on production costs, consider the perceived value to the customer. If your AI tool saves businesses hours of manual work, the price should reflect that savings. Subscription versus one-time payment is another decision point. Subscriptions can provide a steady revenue stream and foster ongoing customer relationships, while one-time payments offer immediate returns. The choice depends on your business model and customer preferences, but flexibility often wins the day.

Strategic partnerships and collaborations can propel your AI business into new realms of success. Collaborating with tech startups can open doors to innovative solutions and fresh perspectives. Perhaps you partner with a startup that complements your strengths, like integrating your AI technology with their user-friendly interface. Alliances with industry experts can also lend credibility and broaden your reach. Imagine your AI tool endorsed by a leading figure in the tech world; it's like having a celebrity chef promote your secret sauce. These partnerships aren't just about expanding reach; they're about enhancing your capabilities and offering customers a more robust solution.

Continuous innovation is the lifeblood of any AI-focused business. AI technology is evolving faster than a cat chasing a laser pointer, and staying ahead requires a commitment to innovation. This means integrating emerging technologies as they develop, ensuring your offerings remain cutting-edge. Encouraging a culture of experimentation and creativity within your team can foster new ideas and drive success. Think of your business as a lab where every idea is worth exploring. These innovations not only keep your product fresh but also maintain your competitive edge, ensuring your business isn't left behind as the AI landscape shifts.

In the grand scheme of things, building a business model around AI is about more than just technology—it's about people, partnerships, and potential. As you lay the foundation for your AI business, consider how you can blend innovation with genuine value, creating solutions that resonate with your audience. Remember, the AI world is vast and ever-changing, but with the right approach, you can carve out your niche and thrive. With a solid business model, you're not just surviving in the AI age; you're setting the stage for the future, where your innovations can shine, and your impact can be felt.

CHAPTER 5
ETHICAL CONSIDERATIONS IN AI

Picture this: you're at a dinner party, and AI is the guest everyone's talking about. It's wearing a tuxedo, dazzling the crowd with tales of its exploits—transforming industries, predicting trends, and even dabbling in art. But, as the conversation deepens, someone raises a glass and asks, "What about ethics?" Suddenly, the room hushes. It's the elephant in the room, the thorny topic that accompanies AI's rise to fame. You see, while AI dazzles with potential, it also treads on thin ethical ice. Understanding AI ethics is like learning to dance on this ice without falling through. It's about balancing innovation with responsibility, ensuring that AI systems serve humanity without running amok.

At the heart of ethical AI are core principles that guide its development and usage. Fairness, transparency, and accountability are the holy trinity of ethical AI. Fairness ensures that AI treats everyone equally, without bias. It's like being impartial in a game of Monopoly, where every player has the same chance to buy Boardwalk. Transparency, on the other hand, is the open book policy. AI decisions should be as clear as a summer sky so users understand how outcomes are reached. Finally, accountability means that someone—be it an individual or organization—owns up when things go awry. It's the grown-up way of saying, "I'll take responsibility for that." These principles create a framework where AI can thrive without trampling on human rights or dignity.

Non-maleficence is another cornerstone of AI ethics, a fancy term for "do no harm." Just as doctors swear an oath to protect their patients, AI developers must ensure their creations don't cause harm. This involves rigorous testing and validation, ensuring AI systems don't inadvertently harm individuals or society. Transparency in decision-making is crucial, allowing users to understand and challenge AI outcomes. Imagine an AI system that's like a secretive magician, pulling rabbits out of hats without revealing the trick. Transparency strips away the mystery, ensuring AI actions are explainable and justifiable.

Ethical AI design is the bedrock upon which responsible AI systems are built. It's about embedding ethical considerations from the get-go, preventing potential harm before it arises. Think of it as installing airbags in a car during manufacturing instead of as an afterthought. Ethical design frameworks provide guidelines, helping developers integrate ethics into every stage of AI development. In research and development, ethics plays a pivotal role in ensuring AI systems are not only efficient but also morally sound. This proactive approach minimizes risks, fostering trust and confidence in AI technologies.

Real-world ethical dilemmas present complex challenges for AI developers and users. Bias in AI algorithms is a prime example, where skewed data can lead to discriminatory outcomes. Imagine an AI hiring system that favors specific demographics over others, perpetuating social inequalities. Privacy concerns also loom large as AI systems collect and process vast amounts of personal data. It's like having a nosy neighbor peeking over the fence, only on a digital scale. These dilemmas highlight the importance of ethical decision-making, ensuring AI serves the greater good without compromising individual rights.

Ethical guidelines and standards are the compass that steers AI towards responsible use. Leading organizations have outlined comprehensive guidelines, such as the Ethics Guidelines for Trustworthy AI by the EU's High-Level Expert Group. These guidelines emphasize human oversight, technical robustness, and diversity, ensuring AI systems are lawful, ethical, and robust. Regulatory frameworks like the AI Act further reinforce these standards, providing a legal backbone for ethical AI deployment. They ensure AI systems respect fundamental rights, promoting fairness and accountability in AI practices. These guidelines and standards are the safety nets, ensuring AI's rise doesn't come at the expense of ethics and morality.

Reflection Section: Ethical Self-Assessment Checklist

Consider your own interactions with AI—whether as a developer, user, or enthusiast. Reflect on the ethical principles that guide your use of AI. Are fairness, transparency, and accountability at the forefront? Use this checklist to evaluate your ethical considerations, identify areas for improvement, and ensure your AI practices align with ethical standards. This exercise will foster a deeper understanding of AI ethics, empowering you to engage with AI responsibly and ethically.

5.1 NAVIGATING ETHICAL CHALLENGES IN AI DEPLOYMENT

Imagine AI as a new employee at your company. It has the potential to become an employee of the month, but it also comes with a set of challenges that need addressing before it starts changing the office decor. One of the biggest hurdles? Data privacy issues. AI applications often process vast amounts of personal data, and mishandling this can be a recipe for disaster. Think of it as a vault that must be kept secure at all costs. Users trust AI with sensitive information, from personal preferences to financial details. If this data leaks or is misused, the consequences can be dire. It's like leaving your wallet at a crowded café and hoping no one takes it. Ensuring that AI respects data privacy is not just a technical challenge but a moral obligation.

Then there's the notorious villain: algorithmic bias. Picture an AI model that, despite its high-tech flair, has a bit of a one-track mind. It tends to favor certain data points, reflecting biases present in the training data. It's like having a friend who insists on only ordering pepperoni pizza because that's all they've ever tried. This bias can perpetuate existing social inequalities, leading to unfair outcomes. For instance, AI used in hiring might favor candidates from specific backgrounds, not because they're the best fit, but because the algorithm was trained on biased data. Addressing this challenge is crucial to ensure AI serves everyone reasonably, without prejudice or favoritism.

To tackle these ethical challenges, implementing bias checks in AI systems is a must. Think of it as regular health check-ups for your AI, ensuring it's not developing any bad habits. These checks involve analyzing the data and algorithms for potential bias-es and adjusting them as needed. It's like teaching your AI to enjoy a variety of pizzas, not just pepperoni. Developing robust data governance policies is another strategy. These policies act as a rulebook, guiding how data is collected, stored, and used. They ensure that all data-handling processes are transparent and accountable, much like a referee ensuring fair play in a sports game.

Consider the case of an AI system deployed in healthcare settings. It's tasked with diagnosing diseases, a responsibility that requires utmost precision and fairness. The developers implemented rigorous bias checks and adhered to strict data governance policies. This approach not only minimized bias but also ensured patient data was handled with care, fostering trust among users. In another example, a financial institution launched transparency initiatives for its AI-driven finance tools. By making AI decision-making processes transparent and understandable, the institution built confidence with its customers, proving that transparency and ethical practices go hand in hand.

Involving diverse stakeholders in AI projects is like assembling a team with varied skills to solve a complex puzzle. It ensures that different perspectives are considered, enhancing the ethical robustness of AI systems. Ethics committees play a vital role here, much like a board of advisors guiding a startup company. They provide oversight, ensuring AI projects adhere to ethical standards. Engaging community feedback is equally important. Users and affected communities can offer valuable insights, highlighting potential ethical issues that developers might overlook. It's a collaborative approach where everyone has a say, ensuring AI development aligns with societal values and expectations.

Navigating the ethical landscape of AI deployment is no small feat. It requires a commitment to addressing challenges, implementing robust strategies, and involving diverse voices. By focusing on these areas, you can ensure that your AI systems not only function efficiently but also uphold the highest ethical standards.

5.2 BALANCING INNOVATION AND RESPONSIBILITY

Imagine you're on a roller coaster, the thrill of innovation rushing through your veins, but there's a sign at the top of the hill reminding you to buckle up. That's the tension between AI innovation and ethics—where speed and excitement can sometimes overshadow the need for safety and responsibility. In the race to develop the next groundbreaking AI application, there's a temptation to prioritize speed over ethical considerations. It's like baking a cake in a hurry and forgetting the sugar; you might finish quickly, but the result won't be satisfying. Ensuring responsible innovation means taking the time to integrate ethics into every stage of AI development. It's about creating systems that not only dazzle with their capabilities but also uphold values of fairness, transparency, and accountability.

Ethical innovation isn't just a noble pursuit; it's a strategic advantage. Companies that weave ethics into their innovation processes build trust and integrity, setting themselves apart in a crowded market. Consider AI startups that have made ethical considerations their selling point. These companies don't just focus on what their AI can do but also on how it does it. They use ethical practices as a competitive edge, attracting customers who value responsible technology. By putting ethics at the forefront, these innovators create a loyal customer base, much like a chef who insists on using only organic ingredients. It's not just about the final dish; it's about the care and integrity that go into making it.

Guidelines for responsible AI innovation are like a recipe for success. Start by incorporating ethics from the outset of your project. This means considering potential ethical implications during the research phase and ensuring that your team is aligned with ethical goals. Continuous ethical evaluation throughout the AI lifecycle is also crucial. It's like checking for seasoning as you cook, making adjustments to ensure the final product is well-balanced. By evaluating ethical considerations at each stage, you can catch potential issues before they become problematic, ensuring your AI systems are both innovative and responsible.

Corporate responsibility plays a pivotal role in supporting ethical AI innovation. Companies that embrace corporate social responsibility (CSR) initiatives often find themselves at the forefront of ethical AI development. These initiatives go beyond profit, focusing on the broader impact of AI on society. They might involve partnerships with ethical organizations, collaborating to ensure AI systems benefit not just the company but also the community. Imagine a tech company partnering with a non-profit to develop AI tools that address social challenges, like improving accessibility for people with disabilities. These collaborations create a ripple effect, demonstrating that AI can be a force for good, positively impacting both organizations and society.

In the world of AI, where the pace of innovation is relentless, balancing responsibility with progress is essential. It's about creating technology that not only pushes boundaries but also respects them. By focusing on ethical innovation, companies can ensure their AI systems are not just cutting-edge but also trust-worthy and beneficial. It's a balancing act, but one that ultimately leads to more sustainable and impactful advancements.

5.3 AI AND SOCIETAL IMPACT: WHAT YOU NEED TO KNOW

Artificial Intelligence is like that new kid on the block who's got everyone talking. It's full of potential but also stirring up a bit of a ruckus. Let's start with the economic transformation. AI has the power to boost productivity and drive innovation at an unprecedented scale. It's like adding rocket fuel to the economy. Whole industries are evolving, and new jobs are sprouting up like mushrooms after the rain. But here's the flip side. As AI takes on more tasks, some traditional jobs might disappear. It's akin to the Industrial Revolution all over again but with robots. Job displacement is real, and it's causing some sleepless nights. Social dynamics are also shifting, thanks to AI. Communication is faster and more efficient, but sometimes less personal. Imagine a world where your best friend is a chatbot. There's a delicate balance between embracing tech and maintaining human connections.

Despite these challenges, AI holds tremendous promise for societal benefit. Take environmental sustainability, for example. AI can analyze vast amounts of data to optimize resource use, reduce waste, and even predict climate patterns. It's like having Mother Nature's personal assistant. Public health is another area ripe for AI intervention. Picture AI-driven solutions that can predict outbreaks, tailor treatments, and even assist in complex surgeries. It's not just about making healthcare more efficient; it's about saving lives. These applications illustrate how AI can be a powerful ally in tackling some of humanity's most pressing issues.

On the other hand, we can't ignore the concerns about AI's social effects. The digital divide is one such issue. While some have the latest tech at their fingertips, others struggle to access even basic digital tools. It's like having a race where some people are on rocket ships while others are on foot. Bridging this gap is crucial to ensure that AI benefits everyone, not just a select few. Then there's AI in law enforcement, a double-edged sword. While it can enhance safety, it also raises ethical questions about surveillance and privacy. Imagine living in a world where every move is watched by an AI eye. These concerns highlight the need for careful consideration of AI's social implications.

Policy and regulation play a vital role in shaping AI's societal impact. Inclusive policy-making ensures that diverse voices are heard, much like a symphony where every instrument counts. Regulations help manage AI's societal effects, providing a framework for responsible use. It's not about stifling innovation; it's about ensuring AI aligns with public interest. Think of it as setting the rules for a fair game where everyone gets a shot at winning. Regulatory approaches must evolve with technology, ensuring they remain relevant and practical. By fostering an environment where innovation thrives within ethical boundaries, we can harness AI's potential for the greater good.

As we wrap up this chapter, remember that AI is more than just a technology; it's a tool that can reshape our world. It's up to us to guide its development responsibly, ensuring it serves as a force for good. With the right balance of innovation, ethics, and regulation, AI can lead us to a future full of possibilities. Now, let's turn the page to explore how AI can enhance productivity in our daily lives.

CHAPTER 6

ENHANCING PRODUCTIVITY WITH AI

Imagine waking up to find that your to-do list has shrunk overnight, miraculously whittled down by a benevolent digital genie. This is not wishful thinking; it's the promise of AI tools designed to streamline your daily tasks, turning chaos into order with the grace of a ballet dancer—albeit one made of code. Whether you're juggling a dozen meetings, drowning in emails, or just trying to find time for a coffee break, AI has you covered. It's like having a personal assistant who never sleeps, doesn't complain, and knows your preferences better than your favorite barista. Let's delve into how AI can transform your day from a series of hurdles into a smooth, efficient journey.

Meet your new best friend: AI-driven email categorization and prioritization tools. These nifty little helpers sort through your inbox with the precision of a librarian on a caffeine high, categorizing messages and flagging the ones that actually matter. Imagine never missing an important email again because your digital assistant has highlighted it for you. Meanwhile, automated meeting schedulers like x.ai or Calendly are revolutionizing how we plan our days. These tools sync with your calendar, sparing you the hassle of endless back-and-forth emails. It's like having a calendar whisperer, arranging your schedule with the ease of a seasoned maître d' seating guests at a fine restaurant.

Time management, once the bane of our existence, is now a breeze thanks to AI-based time-tracking applications. These apps monitor your work habits, providing insights into how you spend your day. It's like having a personal coach who gently nudges you when you're binge-watching cat videos instead of finishing that report. Intelligent calendar management systems take it a step further, integrating tasks and reminders to keep you on track. They ensure you focus on high-priority tasks, leaving you feeling accomplished rather than overwhelmed. With AI managing your time, you can say goodbye to those frantic moments of panic when you realize you've double-booked yourself.

AI also shines in the realm of document management, transforming how we handle files and information. AI-powered document search and indexing tools sift through mountains of paperwork faster than you can say "Ctrl+F," finding exactly what you need in seconds. Automated content summarization tools condense lengthy documents into bite-sized insights, perfect for those who want the gist without wading through text. Real-time collaborative editing platforms are the cherry on top, allowing teams to work together seamlessly, no matter where they are in the world. It's like having a digital office where everyone's on the same page—literally.

In customer interaction, AI is the star performer, handling inquiries with the charm of a seasoned diplomat. AI chatbots respond to customer questions around the clock, providing instant support without the need for coffee breaks. These bots are trained to handle FAQs, troubleshoot issues, and even upsell products, all while maintaining a friendly persona. It's like having a customer service team that never sleeps, ensuring that your clients always feel heard. Automated FAQ systems further enhance this experience, allowing customers to find answers to common questions without waiting in line. These systems improve response times and service quality, making your business as efficient as a well-oiled machine.

Reflection Section: AI Productivity Checklist

Take a moment to evaluate your current productivity setup. Consider the following: Are there tasks that could be automated? Which AI tools could enhance your workflow? Use this checklist to identify opportunities for integrating AI into your daily routine, ensuring you get the most out of your time and resources. This exercise will help you pinpoint areas for improvement, setting the stage for a more efficient and productive day.

6.1 INCORPORATING AI INTO PROJECT MANAGEMENT

Consider AI-enhanced project management tools your trusty sidekick, swooping in to save the day when deadlines loom and chaos reigns. These digital wizards help streamline planning, monitoring, and execution, making sure every cog in the machine turns smoothly. With AI-based project timeline optimization, you can anticipate bottlenecks before they even form. It's like having a crystal ball that predicts the future, ensuring tasks are completed on schedule without the usual stress. Resource allocation and workload balancing tools take the guesswork out of who should do what and when, optimizing team productivity by distributing tasks based on each member's capacity and expertise. Picture it as your own project manager—minus the coffee addiction and penchant for sticky notes.

Risk management in projects can feel like a high-stakes poker game, with the potential for disaster lurking around every corner. Enter AI to tilt the odds in your favor. With predictive analytics, AI assesses potential risks by analyzing data patterns and trends, providing insights that help you make informed decisions when uncertainty is high. It's like having a seasoned gambler whispering the odds in your ear. Automated contingency planning systems further bolster your defenses, crafting backup plans for when things go sideways. AI evaluates various scenarios, allowing you to prepare for the unexpected and mitigate risks before they spiral out of control. This proactive approach turns potential setbacks into manageable challenges, ensuring your projects stay on track.

Team collaboration can sometimes resemble herding cats, with everyone scattered and out of sync. AI swoops in with tools that enhance communication and cooperation, bringing order to the chaos. AI-driven communication platforms, such as Slack integrations, ensure that all team members stay connected and informed, fostering a collaborative atmosphere even when miles apart. Automated task assignment and progress tracking streamline the workflow, allowing team leaders to assign tasks efficiently and monitor progress in real-time. It's like having an air traffic controller directing the flow of work, ensuring everyone knows what to do and when. This transparency and organization promote a more cohesive team dynamic, boosting morale and productivity.

Consider the case of a software development company that implemented AI-driven project management tools to streamline its processes. By optimizing timelines and balancing workloads, the company not only reduced project completion times but also improved team satisfaction. Developers could focus on coding rather than juggling multiple responsibilities, resulting in higher-quality software delivered on time. In the realm of construction, AI has proven its worth by enhancing project management outcomes. A construction firm employed AI for risk assessment and automated planning, leading to a significant reduction in cost overruns and delays. The AI identified potential risks like weather disruptions and supply chain issues, allowing the firm to adjust plans proactively. This forward-thinking approach transformed the company's projects from reactive firefighting to strategic execution, illustrating AI's potential to revolutionize project management across industries.

6.2 AI-ENHANCED DECISION MAKING

Imagine having a superpower that lets you peek into the future, helping you make decisions that turn out to be spot-on every time. This isn't a plot from a sci-fi novel; it's what AI's role in decision support systems offers. AI-powered business intelligence platforms are like having a team of analysts working tirelessly, crunching numbers, and spitting out insights faster than you can say "spreadsheet." These platforms digest vast amounts of data, transforming it into visualizations that are easy to understand and act upon. Real-time data analysis tools take this a step further by providing up-to-the-minute insights, allowing you to make informed decisions on the fly. They're like the GPS of decision-making, recalculating your route as new information surfaces.

Predictive analytics is another feather in AI's cap, enabling businesses to forecast trends and make strategic decisions with confidence. It's like having a crystal ball that actually works. Market trend prediction tools analyze historical data and current market conditions to forecast what's coming next, helping you stay ahead of the curve. Meanwhile, customer behavior analysis systems delve into consumer habits, predicting preferences and tailoring experiences to individual needs. This insight is invaluable for businesses looking to enhance customer satisfaction and boost loyalty. By leveraging predictive analytics, you can anticipate changes and adapt your strategy, ensuring you're always one step ahead of the competition.

In the financial world, AI is the savvy investor you never knew you needed. It optimizes financial decision-making by analyzing market data and trends to inform investment strategies. Algorithmic trading platforms use AI to execute trades at lightning speed, capitalizing on market fluctuations faster than any human could. These platforms assess risk and potential reward, ensuring your investments are both strategic and calculated. On the budgeting side, AI-driven financial forecasting models take the guesswork out of planning. They analyze past performance and current conditions to predict future economic outcomes, helping businesses allocate resources more effectively and avoid unpleasant surprises. It's like having a financial advisor who's always on call, never takes a commission, and is really good with numbers.

Operational decision-making is another domain where AI flexes its muscles, improving efficiency and resource allocation in businesses. AI tools for supply chain optimization evaluate logistics, identifying the most efficient routes and schedules to minimize costs and maximize efficiency. They're like a chess grandmaster, planning several moves ahead to ensure everything falls into place. Automated maintenance scheduling systems predict when equipment will need servicing, reducing downtime and preventing costly breakdowns. This proactive approach ensures that operations run smoothly, much like a well-oiled machine, without the late-night panic when something unexpectedly goes awry.

AI-enhanced decision-making isn't just a tool; it's a game-changer. By providing insights and recommendations based on data, it empowers businesses to operate more efficiently and strategically. Whether you're navigating market trends, crafting financial strategies, or optimizing operations, AI is the partner that turns decisions into opportunities. It's like having a trusted advisor who's always ready with the correct answer, helping you make choices that drive success and growth.

6.3 MAXIMIZING EFFICIENCY WITH AI-ASSISTED WORKFLOWS

Picture your workday as a tangled ball of yarn and AI as the deft fingers unraveling it into a neat, usable strand. AI-assisted workflows are those nimble fingers streamlining processes and transforming the chaos into a seamless operation. They combine the computational muscle of AI with everyday tasks to automate repetitive actions, reduce manual errors, and enhance productivity. What makes these workflows tick? The key components are algorithms, data, and integration. Algorithms are the brains processing data with precision. Data provides the raw material, and integration ensures these elements work harmoniously within your existing systems. Together, they form a robust framework that boosts efficiency and accuracy, doing the heavy lifting so you can focus on strategic initiatives.

In a world where time is money, AI in workflow automation acts like a supercharged engine, propelling tasks with minimal human intervention. Take automated data entry, for example. It's like having a diligent assistant who never tires, inputting information into systems with speed and precision that no human can match. AI doesn't just stop at entry; it processes data, too, sifting through it to extract valuable insights. Workflow management tools equipped with AI capabilities further enhance this process. They coordinate tasks, manage schedules, and ensure that everything runs like clockwork. By automating these complex workflows, businesses can reduce errors, speed up operations, and free up human resources for more creative and strategic endeavors.

Efficiency isn't just about speed; it's about optimizing processes, too. AI excels at identifying bottlenecks and suggesting improvements, much like a savvy consultant who spots inefficiencies a mile away. AI-driven process mapping and analysis tools provide a bird's-eye view of your operations, highlighting areas where tasks slow down, or resources are underutilized. These insights allow for continuous improvement as AI feedback loops gather data on performance and suggest iterative enhancements. It's like having a coach who constantly analyzes your play, offering tips to fine-tune your strategy. This dynamic approach ensures workflows remain agile and responsive, adapting to changing demands and maximizing productivity.

Real-world applications of AI-assisted workflows are as diverse as they are impressive. In healthcare, AI revolutionizes patient management workflows. By automating administrative tasks like scheduling and billing, healthcare providers can focus more on patient care. AI-driven systems also streamline data management, ensuring that medical records are up-to-date and accessible, reducing wait times and improving service quality. In the manufacturing sector, AI optimizes production line workflows by monitoring equipment and predicting maintenance needs. This proactive approach minimizes downtime, enhances safety, and boosts output. Companies employing AI in their workflows often find themselves with a competitive edge, as these systems not only improve efficiency but also enhance the overall quality of their offerings.

As AI continues to evolve, its role in maximizing workflow efficiency becomes more vital. By integrating AI into daily operations, businesses can operate with greater precision and flexibility. This transformation not only enhances productivity but also positions organizations to thrive in an ever-competitive landscape. With AI's ability to streamline and optimize, the future of work looks sharper, brighter, and more efficient than ever before.

MAKE A DIFFERENCE WITH YOUR REVIEW
UNLOCK THE POWER OF GENEROSITY

"The best way to find yourself is to lose yourself in the service of others."

MAHATMA GANDHI.

People who give without expecting anything in return live happier lives. So, let's make a difference together!

Would you help someone just like you who is curious about AI and how it can make life easier but unsure where to start?

My mission is to make learning about AI simple and exciting for everyone.

But to reach more people, I need your help.

Most people choose books based on reviews. So, I'm asking you to help a fellow AI explorer by leaving a review.

It costs nothing and takes less than a minute, but your review could change someone's AI journey.

...one more small business create fantastic content for their community. ...one more entrepreneur use AI to support their family. ...one more employee find fulfilling work with AI skills. ...one more person discover new growth and opportunities.

To make a difference, simply scan the QR code below and leave a review:

QR code

If you love helping others, you're my kind of person. Thank you from the bottom of my heart!

Ken Kimberley

CHAPTER 7

OVERCOMING LEARNING BARRIERS

Picture yourself standing at the base of a mountain, staring up at the summit cloaked in mist. That summit represents mastering AI, and the climb? Well, that's where the challenge and the fun begin. For many, the path is littered with intimidating jargon and complex theories that make AI feel like it's speaking in tongues. But fear not; this chapter is your trusty guide, equipped with a map to simplify those seemingly impenetrable concepts. Consider AI as a new language, similar to learning to speak "tech" fluently. Before you know it, you'll be chatting in algorithms and models like a native speaker.

7.1 SIMPLIFYING AI CONCEPTS FOR BEGINNERS

Let's start by tackling those head-scratching terms thrown around in AI circles. Imagine AI as a bustling city, with machine learning as the public transportation system, whisking data from place to place. In this analogy, algorithms are the routes guiding data along its journey. Think of an algorithm as a recipe, a set of instructions that the AI follows to solve problems. When someone mentions "models," don't picture runway models strutting in high fashion; instead, visualize blueprints that the AI uses to predict outcomes based on data patterns. And datasets? They're the ingredients—collections of data that fuel AI's decision-making process. By breaking down these terms into everyday language, we can demystify AI, making it as approachable as a cup of coffee on a lazy Sunday morning.

Now, let's illuminate some core concepts in the AI universe. Supervised learning is like having a personal tutor who guides AI with labeled examples, teaching it to recognize patterns and make predictions. Meanwhile, unsupervised learning is AI's version of self-discovery, exploring data without labels to uncover hidden structures. It's like letting a curious child loose in a library, where they create their understanding from the books around them. At the heart of these processes are AI models, structured like decision trees, neural networks, or regression lines, each with its unique way of processing and learning from data. These models are the brains of AI, turning raw data into insights and actions, much like how our brains process stimuli and make decisions.

Visual aids can be your best friends in this learning adventure, especially when tackling abstract AI concepts. Flowcharts, for instance, can unravel the labyrinth of AI decision-making, illustrating how data flows through an algorithm like a river meandering through a valley. Infographics serve as visual storytellers, explaining how data input transforms into valuable output, akin to spinning straw into gold. These tools don't just simplify complex ideas; they make them tangible, like turning a theoretical concept into a hands-on experiment. By leaning on these visual representations, you can see AI's inner workings with clarity, making abstract concepts as clear as a summer's day.

To solidify your understanding, let's dive into some step-by-step examples. Imagine AI as a chef preparing a dish. First, it gathers ingredients—data—from the pantry. Next, it follows a recipe—an algorithm—to mix and cook these ingredients, transforming them into a delicious meal—an actionable insight. A practical scenario might involve AI predicting the weather. It starts by collecting historical weather data (ingredients), analyzes patterns using algorithms (recipes), and finally predicts tomorrow's weather (the dish). This concrete example shows AI's problem-solving prowess, demonstrating how it processes information to deliver solutions. By walking through these examples, you can grasp the "how" and "why" behind AI's decision-making, turning theoretical knowledge into practical skills.

Visual Element: AI Decision-Making Flowchart

To further enhance your understanding, take a moment to study an AI decision-making flowchart. This visual guide maps out the journey from data input to actionable insight, illustrating each step with clarity. By following the flowchart, you can see how AI navigates decisions, reinforcing your grasp of its processes. This exercise will help you visualize AI's inner workings, bridging the gap between abstract theory and practical application.

7.2 CREATING A PERSONALIZED AI LEARNING PATH

Imagine you're at a buffet, and AI is the feast laid out before you. Just like you wouldn't pile your plate with everything at once, learning AI is best approached by understanding what suits your taste and style. Are you a visual learner who thrives on diagrams and videos? Perhaps you prefer auditory learning, soaking up knowledge through podcasts and lectures. Or maybe you're kinesthetic, needing hands-on projects to truly grasp concepts.

Knowing your learning style is like having a personalized menu, and there are self-assessment tools online to help you identify it. By tailoring your AI learning experience to your preferred style, you make the process not only practical but also enjoyable. It's like choosing a playlist for your workout; when the right tunes play, the miles fly by.

Setting clear and achievable goals is your map in the AI landscape, preventing you from wandering aimlessly. Think of goals as the milestones on your path, guiding your progress and keeping you motivated. Creating SMART goals—those that are Specific, Measurable, Achievable, Relevant, and Time-bound—can transform vague aspirations into concrete plans. For instance, instead of saying, "I want to learn AI," specify your intention: "I will complete an introductory course in machine learning by the end of next month." Establish both short-term and long-term milestones, much like planning a road trip with stops along the way. These checkpoints help you track progress, celebrate achievements, and adjust your route as needed. Remember, a journey of a thousand miles begins with a single step—and a well-marked map.

Curating resources tailored to your needs is like having a well-stocked toolbox. With so many online courses, tutorials, books, and articles available, it can feel overwhelming. Fear not, for the key is to select resources that align with your learning style and level. Beginner-friendly courses like those found on Coursera or edX can provide a structured introduction, while tutorials on platforms like YouTube offer bite-sized insights that fit into a busy schedule. For foundational knowledge, books such as "AI for Dummies" or articles from reputable sites like Towards Data Science can be invaluable. This curated approach ensures you're not just consuming information but absorbing it, turning theory into practice. It's about finding the right tools for the task at hand, ensuring you're building a solid foundation without getting buried in information overload.

Implementing adaptive learning techniques can be your secret weapon in mastering AI. These strategies adjust to your progress and challenges, much like a personal trainer who tailors workouts to your evolving fitness level. AI-powered learning platforms, such as Duolingo's approach to language learning, use algorithms to provide personalized feedback, helping you focus on areas that need improvement. This adaptive learning style mimics the very technology you're studying, using data to enhance learning efficiency. Regular self-assessment and reflection are also crucial, acting like a rear-view mirror to gauge how far you've come and what lies ahead. By incorporating these techniques, you create a dynamic learning environment that evolves with you, ensuring you're always moving forward, even when the road gets a little bumpy.

7.3 EFFICIENT TIME MANAGEMENT FOR AI MASTERY

Picture this: you're juggling work, family, friends, and now the ambitious goal of learning AI. It's like trying to balance a stack of plates while riding a unicycle. But fear not because efficient time management is the key to keeping everything spinning smoothly. Let's kick things off with some tried-and-true techniques that can help you carve out time for AI without sacrificing your sanity. The Pomodoro Technique is a favorite among productivity enthusiasts, where you work in focused bursts of 25 minutes followed by a short break. It's like a workout for your brain, keeping it sharp and preventing burnout. Then there's the Eisenhower Box, a method that involves categorizing tasks based on urgency and importance. Imagine it as your personal sorting hat for daily responsibilities, helping you prioritize AI learning without getting overwhelmed by the less critical stuff.

Crafting a balanced learning schedule is like designing a workout plan tailored to your needs. You wouldn't hit the gym without a plan, and the same goes for AI studies. Start by laying out a weekly study plan that allocates specific time slots for different AI topics. It's essential to find a rhythm that accommodates your personal and professional responsibilities. Life is unpredictable, and a rigid schedule can lead to frustration. Flexibility is your friend, allowing you to adjust your learning pace based on progress. So, if you need an extra day to wrap your head around neural networks, take it! The key is consistency, not perfection. With a realistic and adaptable schedule, you're more likely to stick with it, making AI learning a rewarding part of your routine rather than a chore.

Why not let AI itself lend a hand in optimizing your study sessions? AI-based apps for scheduling and productivity tracking can become your personal time-management assistants. These tools help you plan your days efficiently, ensuring you allocate enough time for deep learning sessions. Imagine an AI assistant like Sunsama or Notion sending you automated reminders and study prompts. It's like having a digital coach cheering you on and keeping you accountable. By leveraging these tools, you can streamline your learning processes, focus on high-impact tasks, and even sneak in a little time for those Netflix binges guilt-free. AI isn't just what you're learning—it's also a powerful ally that helps you learn more effectively.

Let's talk about distractions, the bane of productivity. Creating a dedicated study environment is crucial for maintaining focus. Whether it's a cozy corner with a comfy chair or a sleek desk with minimal clutter, find a space that signals your brain it's time to learn. Keep distractions at bay by using digital tools designed to block tempting websites. Extensions like Freedom or StayFocusd can help you resist the siren call of social media and aimless online surfing. It's like putting blinders on a racehorse, keeping you on track and laser-focused. By setting boundaries and reducing distractions, you give AI learning your full attention, turning study sessions into immersive experiences.

7.4 FINDING COMMUNITY SUPPORT IN AI LEARNING

In the vast and sometimes bewildering world of AI, finding a community can feel like discovering a hidden oasis. Online AI communities are teeming with enthusiasts and experts ready to share their knowledge and support. Dive into forums like Reddit's r/MachineLearning or Stack Overflow, where AI discussions are as vibrant as a bustling marketplace. These platforms allow you to ask questions, share experiences, and learn from the collective wisdom of people who have been where you are now. Social media groups dedicated to AI can also be invaluable. They offer a space for real-time interaction and updates, connecting you with a global network of learners and professionals eager to explore AI's endless possibilities. The camaraderie and shared passion in these groups make learning feel less like a solo expedition and more like a team adventure.

Engaging with collaborative learning platforms adds another layer to your AI education. Think of these platforms as interactive classrooms where teamwork makes the dream work. Online workshops and hackathons are excellent opportunities to apply what you've learned in a dynamic environment. They push you out of your comfort zone, encouraging you to think on your feet and collaborate with others. Virtual study groups and peer mentoring systems provide a supportive framework where you can discuss concepts, troubleshoot problems, and celebrate successes together. The beauty of these platforms lies in their ability to foster a sense of community, even in a virtual space. They remind you that while AI might sometimes feel like a solitary endeavor, you're never truly alone in the learning process.

Networking with fellow AI enthusiasts and professionals can unlock doors you didn't even know existed. Attending AI conferences and webinars offers access to cutting-edge insights and trends, as well as the chance to rub elbows with industry leaders. These events are not just about absorbing information; they're about building relationships. Local AI meetups and interest groups provide a more intimate setting for networking, allowing you to connect with others in your area who share your passion for AI. These interactions can lead to collaborations, job opportunities, or simply a new friend who understands your excitement about the latest AI breakthrough. Networking is like planting seeds; you might not see immediate results, but over time, those connections can blossom into valuable professional relationships.

Finding a mentor can be a game-changer in your AI learning experience. A mentor offers guidance, shares insights, and helps you navigate the complexities of AI. Platforms such as LinkedIn or specialized mentorship programs provide access to individuals who are willing to share their expertise. When approaching potential mentors, it's important to be genuine and respectful. Express your interest in learning from them, and be clear about what you hope to gain from the mentorship. Remember, mentorship is a two-way street; be open to feedback and willing to show your appreciation for their time and support. With the right mentor, you can accelerate your learning, gain unique perspectives, and develop the confidence to tackle even the most challenging AI concepts.

CHAPTER 8

AI TOOLS AND RESOURCES

Picture this: you're a chef in a bustling kitchen, and everyone is waiting for your culinary masterpiece. Only your ingredients are missing, and the pot is empty. Enter AI tools, your digital sous-chefs, ready to slice, dice, and stir up a storm of productivity. These tools are the secret ingredients turning beginners into seasoned pros, no matter the field. Whether you're a budding entrepreneur or an art aficionado, AI offers the cutting-edge resources needed to spice up your projects. Let's dive into the essential AI tools that are user-friendly enough for beginners yet powerful enough to impress even the most tech-savvy of us.

For those looking to explore AI in mobile and embedded devices, TensorFlow Lite is your new best friend. Imagine it as the Swiss Army knife of AI tools—compact, versatile, and ready to handle a multitude of tasks. TensorFlow Lite is designed to bring the power of machine learning to your pocket, running models directly on your mobile device with lightning-fast speed. It's like having a mini AI lab in your smartphone, capable of everything from image recognition to natural language processing. The best part? It's optimized for performance, so your device won't start acting like it just ran a marathon.

Then there's Google's Teachable Machine, a tool so intuitive it practically holds your hand through the process of creating machine learning models. It's the perfect playground for those just dipping their toes into the world of AI. With Teachable Machine, you don't need to code or have a PhD in computer science. Simply upload your data, and the tool helps you design, train, and deploy models in a snap. You could teach it to recognize your favorite snack or distinguish between your cat's meows and demands for food. It's a creative tinkerer's dream, offering endless possibilities without the steep learning curve.

Now, let's talk about user-friendly interfaces that make AI accessible to everyone. IBM Watson Studio offers a drag-and-drop interface that transforms complex data science tasks into something akin to playing with building blocks. You can assemble models and workflows without writing a single line of code, making it ideal for those who'd rather not wrestle with syntax errors. It's like having a co-pilot who takes care of the heavy lifting while you steer toward discovery. RunwayML is another gem in the AI toolkit, especially for creatives. This tool lets you generate stunning visuals and inventive designs with minimal effort. It's like having an AI-powered art assistant ready to bring your visions to life with just a few clicks.

For those looking to delve into data analysis and creative content generation, RapidMiner and Magenta Studio are your go-to tools. RapidMiner turns data mining into a walk in the park, handling complex analyses with the ease of a seasoned detective piecing together a mystery. It's perfect for anyone who wants to uncover hidden insights without getting bogged down in technical jargon. Meanwhile, Magenta Studio uses AI to compose music, providing a fresh twist on the creative process. With it, you can orchestrate melodies and harmonies that resonate with emotion, all while sipping your morning coffee.

Getting started with these tools is simpler than assembling furniture with a trusty instruction manual. For TensorFlow Lite, begin by downloading the software development kit (SDK) and following the step-by-step installation guide. You'll be up and running faster than you can say "neural network." With Teachable Machine, jump in by visiting the website, where tutorials guide you through the model creation process. IBM Watson Studio and RunwayML both offer beginner tutorials that walk you through the basics, ensuring you're not left scratching your head. RapidMiner and Magenta Studio provide detailed setup instructions, making it easy for first-time users to hit the ground running.

Interactive Element: AI Tool Checklist

To make the most of these resources, create a checklist of the tools you want to explore. Note their key features and potential applications in your projects. As you experiment, jot down your thoughts and experiences. This checklist will help you track your progress and ensure you're getting the most out of your AI toolkit.

8.1 EXPLORING FREE AI RESOURCES ONLINE

AI education doesn't have to break the bank. In fact, there's a buffet of free resources out there, ready to serve anyone hungry for knowledge. Coursera and edX, for instance, are like the all-you-can-eat buffets of the online learning world. They offer a range of courses from top universities that cover everything from the basics of AI to more intricate machine learning concepts, all at no cost. Coursera's free AI and machine learning courses are particularly popular, providing a solid foundation in AI principles. Meanwhile, edX serves up courses from prestigious institutions, allowing you to learn from the best without stepping foot on a campus. It's like having the professors come to your living room, minus the hefty tuition fees.

Open-source AI libraries are another treasure trove for the budding AI enthusiast. Take Scikit-learn, for example. This handy tool is perfect for data analysis, offering a range of functions for building and evaluating machine learning models. It's like having a Swiss Army knife for data tasks, and the best part? It's free. Then there's Keras, an open-source library designed for deep learning applications. Keras acts as a friendly interface for complex tasks, allowing you to build deep learning models with ease. It's the equivalent of a friendly neighbor who not only lends you their lawnmower but also offers to help mow the lawn. These libraries provide access to powerful tools and frameworks, leveling the playing field for anyone eager to dive into AI.

Data is the lifeblood of AI, and having access to quality datasets is crucial for practice and project development. Luckily, platforms like Kaggle offer public datasets, providing a playground for those wanting to test their skills and build new projects. Kaggle's datasets cover a wide range of topics, from housing prices to health indicators, giving you the chance to tackle real-world problems. The UCI Machine Learning Repository is another fantastic source, offering datasets that have been used in countless research projects. It's like a well-stocked library where every book is a potential project waiting to happen. Google Dataset Search is also a go-to resource, acting as a digital librarian that helps you find datasets across the web. Whether you're looking to train a model or simply explore data, these resources offer a wealth of material to get started.

Community-driven resources are the backbone of learning and support in the AI world. GitHub is a prime example, hosting countless repositories for collaborative coding and project sharing. It's a bit like a giant workshop where everyone is tinkering with their own projects but is always ready to lend a hand or share a tool. Platforms like DrivenData host AI challenges and competitions, offering not just the chance to win prizes but also the opportunity to learn and collaborate with others. These competitions are like hackathons where you can test your skills, learn from others, and even contribute to meaningful projects. Engaging in these communities not only enhances your knowledge but also connects you with like-minded individuals who share your passion for AI.

8.2 BUILDING YOUR AI TOOLKIT: SOFTWARE AND PLATFORMS

Getting into AI is like setting up a home gym. It would help if you had the right equipment to work out those brain muscles effectively. Let's start with two heavy hitters in AI development: Anaconda and Jupyter Notebook. Anaconda is an all-in-one solution for managing AI and data science projects. Think of it as your gym membership, offering access to a wealth of tools and libraries in one neat package. It's the go-to platform for installing Python, R, and their myriad libraries, ensuring you spend less time wrestling with installations and more time flexing your data skills. Anaconda simplifies package management and deployment, making it a breeze to switch between different environments for your projects. Whether you're dabbling in data analysis or diving into deep learning, Anaconda provides a stable foundation to build upon.

Jupyter Notebook, on the other hand, is like your personal training log. It's an interactive coding environment where you can write code, visualize data, and document your findings all in one place. Imagine a digital notebook that seamlessly integrates execution and explanation. You can experiment with code, visualize the output with graphs and charts, and then annotate it with markdown text, creating a comprehensive record of your work. Jupyter is particularly beloved by data scientists and researchers for its ability to combine narrative, code, and visuals in a single document, making it easier to explore data and share insights. Whether you're developing machine learning models or conducting exploratory data analysis, Jupyter Notebook keeps everything organized and accessible.

For those looking to scale up, cloud-based AI platforms offer the flexibility and power needed for larger projects. Google Cloud AI Platform is a fantastic choice for those wanting to harness the power of the cloud. It's like renting a high-end gym with all the fancy equipment you could dream of. Google Cloud provides a suite of AI tools and services, from pre-trained models to custom model training and deployment. It offers a robust infrastructure that can handle the demands of big data and complex computations, allowing you to scale your AI projects without breaking a sweat. Plus, with integrated tools for data labeling, automated machine learning, and model serving, the Google Cloud AI Platform streamlines the entire AI workflow.

Amazon SageMaker is another cloud-based powerhouse designed for end-to-end machine learning. Picture it as the personal trainer who not only guides you through the exercises but also tracks your progress and suggests improvements. Sage-Maker simplifies the process of building, training, and deploying machine learning models at scale. It provides an intuitive interface and a range of pre-built algorithms, making it accessible for beginners while still offering deep customization for advanced users. With features like one-click training and deployment, Sage-Maker takes the hassle out of managing infrastructure, allowing you to focus on developing and refining your models.

When it comes to coding environments, Integrated Development Environments (IDEs) are your best friends. PyCharm is the IDE of choice for Python-based AI development. It's like having a personal coach who keeps you on track and error-free. PyCharm offers a rich set of features, including code completion, syntax highlighting, and debugging tools, all tailored to Python's unique quirks. It's designed to boost productivity and reduce the time spent troubleshooting code, making it ideal for AI developers who want to stay focused on their projects. Meanwhile, Visual Studio Code, with its versatile extensions for AI, is a favorite among developers who value flexibility. It's like a Swiss Army knife, adaptable to a wide range of programming tasks. With extensions for Python, Jupyter, and TensorFlow, VS Code transforms into a robust AI development environment, offering features like integrated terminals, version control, and more.

Choosing the right tools for your AI projects is crucial, much like picking the right workout gear. Start by assessing your specific needs and project goals. Consider factors like ease of use, scalability, and community support. Compare features and functionalities to ensure the tools align with your requirements. For instance, if you're just starting, opt for tools with user-friendly interfaces and strong documentation. If you're working on large-scale projects, prioritize tools that offer scalability and robust support. By carefully selecting your AI toolkit, you'll set yourself up for success, ensuring that your projects run smoothly and efficiently.

8.3 LEVERAGING ONLINE COURSES AND TUTORIALS

So, you're ready to dive into the world of AI, but the sheer volume of courses out there makes it feel like trying to choose a movie on Netflix with a group of friends—endless options and differing opinions. Fear not! Let's talk about some top-tier courses that cater to both newcomers and those looking to deepen their AI knowledge. Andrew Ng's Machine Learning course on Coursera is like the blockbuster hit of online AI education. Designed by one of the pioneers in the field, it covers everything from the basics to more complex machine learning algorithms. Ng's approachable teaching style makes even the trickiest concepts digestible, ensuring that you're not just learning but understanding. Then there's Fast.AI's Practical Deep Learning for Coders. This course is a favorite for those who prefer jumping into the deep end. It's hands-on from the get-go, allowing you to start building models quickly, and it's a fantastic way to see theory in action. Both courses offer a structured path to AI mastery, making them perfect for different learning styles and paces.

Now, for those who learn best by doing rather than just watching slides, interactive tutorials, and workshops are your best bet. Codecademy's interactive AI tutorials are like a choose-your-own-adventure book for coding. They provide a guided yet exploratory experience, allowing you to write and test code in real-time. It's the perfect playground for those eager to get their hands dirty without fear of breaking anything. Similarly, Kaggle's workshops for Python and machine learning offer an arena to hone your skills through practical exercises and competitions. Imagine a coding boot camp where you can pace yourself, gaining immediate feedback as you tackle real-world problems. These experiences not only solidify your learning but also boost your confidence as you see your skills develop right before your eyes.

Choosing the right course is a bit like dating—you want something that matches your needs and complements your strengths. Start by evaluating the course content. Does it cover the topics you're interested in? Is the instructor someone who knows their stuff and can explain it well? Look for courses that balance theory with practical application, offering projects or labs where you can apply what you've learned. It's not just about listening to lectures; it's about engaging with the material and making it your own. Consider the course format and time commitment, too. Are you looking for something intensive or a course you can fit around your busy schedule? By aligning these factors with your personal learning objectives and current skill level, you ensure a fruitful and enjoyable educational experience.

In the rapidly evolving world of AI, staying current is as vital as that morning cup of coffee. Continuous learning isn't just a buzzword; it's a necessity. Subscribing to AI newsletters and blogs is a fantastic way to keep your finger on the pulse of the latest trends and breakthroughs. They're like your daily dose of AI news, delivered right to your inbox. Participating in webinars and online conferences offers another layer of engagement, connecting you with experts and peers from around the globe. These events not only provide fresh perspectives but also allow you to ask questions and join discussions, enhancing your understanding and sparking new ideas. The beauty of these resources is that they're often free or low-cost, making them accessible to anyone eager to expand their AI horizons.

As we explore these educational avenues, the key takeaway is clear: AI education is more accessible than ever, thanks to a wealth of online resources tailored to different needs and skill levels. With the right courses and continuous learning, you're not just preparing for the future—you're shaping it. Next, we'll delve into how you can apply this knowledge to real-world projects, turning theory into practice and ideas into innovations.

CHAPTER 9

VISUAL AIDS AND INTERACTIVE LEARNING

Picture this: you're trying to navigate the labyrinthine world of AI with nothing but a flashlight and a vague map. It's like trying to find your way out of an escape room blindfolded. That's where visual aids come in, acting as your guiding stars in the vast cosmos of artificial intelligence. They break down complex concepts into digestible pieces, transforming confusion into clarity. Think of visual aids as your AI compass, pointing the way toward understanding without the need for a PhD in computer science.

9.1 VISUALIZING AI CONCEPTS WITH DIAGRAMS

Let's talk diagrams. They're a bit like those IKEA instructions but without the missing screws and confusing arrows. Diagrams have this magical ability to take the convoluted and make it understandable. They simplify AI concepts by visually breaking them down, making even the most challenging ideas approachable. Flowcharts, for instance, can illuminate AI decision-making processes, showing you exactly how an AI reaches its conclusions step by step. Imagine following a flowchart that guides you through how an AI decides whether to recommend a cat video or a dog meme—it's all about the branching paths of logic. Then, there are network diagrams, which lay bare the intricate architectures of neural networks. These diagrams reveal how data travels through layers of a neural network, much like a train journey with stops at various stations, each refining the input into something meaningful.

Creating effective diagrams is an art form, and like any art, it requires a few key techniques. First, there's color coding—your best friend in differentiating concepts. A splash of color can highlight relationships and distinctions, making it easier to follow the narrative of a diagram. Imagine using blue for input data, green for processing stages, and red for output—instantly, the diagram becomes more intuitive. Labeling is another essential tool. Clear, concise labels act like tour guides, explaining what each part of the diagram represents. They prevent confusion and ensure that anyone—whether they're new to AI or an old hand—can understand the story being told.

Now, let's showcase some examples where diagrams work their magic. Infographic-style diagrams can transform data processing workflows into something you'd want to hang on your wall. They combine visuals with data, making complex processes seem as simple as assembling a sandwich. Meanwhile, step-by-step visual breakdowns of machine learning algorithms provide a clear pathway through the forest of data and code. These diagrams demystify the inner workings of algorithms, showing how they learn and adapt over time. It's like watching a time-lapse of a seed growing into a mighty oak—fascinating and illuminating.

For those itching to create their own diagrams, several tools can make the process as smooth as a hot knife through butter. Lucidchart is a fantastic choice for collaborative design. It's like having a digital whiteboard where you and your team can sketch, share, and refine diagrams in real-time. Want something a bit more user-friendly? Canva offers easy-to-use templates that let you whip up diagrams without breaking a sweat. It's perfect for when you need to create something visually stunning but don't have hours to spare. These tools empower you to become the cartographer of your AI journey, mapping out concepts in a way that's both engaging and enlightening.

Visual Element: Diagramming Challenge

Create a flowchart that outlines how ChatGPT processes a prompt. Start with the input stage, move through processing, and end with output. Use color coding and labels to enhance clarity. Share your diagram with peers for feedback and see how different perspectives can improve understanding.

Interactive Exercises for Hands-On Learning

Imagine trying to learn to ride a bicycle by reading a manual. Sure, you could memorize the instructions, but until you hop on and pedal, you won't really get it. That's the magic of interactive exercises—they're like the training wheels of the learning world. They allow you to engage directly with AI concepts, making the abstract tangible and the complex manageable. In the realm of AI, hands-on learning is invaluable. It transforms passive absorption into active participation, reinforcing your understanding through practice. Platforms like LeetCode offer interactive coding challenges that put your skills to the test, allowing you to solve problems in real time. It's like a digital playground where you can experiment without fear of judgment. Meanwhile, AI simulation exercises let you practice real-world scenarios, providing a safe environment to apply what you've learned. It's one thing to know the theory behind AI; it's another to see it in action.

Creating effective interactive exercises is an art that requires a thoughtful approach. Start by designing tasks that cater to various learning styles. Scenario-based problem-solving tasks are excellent for those who thrive on real-world applications. They take you through situations you might encounter in everyday life, helping you see AI's relevance and utility. Step-by-step guided simulations, on the other hand, break down complex processes into manageable chunks, allowing learners to progress at their own pace. This method ensures that everyone, regardless of their starting point, can grasp the material and build confidence as they go. The key is to make these exercises engaging and educational, striking a balance between challenge and support.

Consider some stellar examples of interactive learning that have proven effective in teaching AI. Build-your-own AI model tutorials guide you through creating simple models from scratch, demystifying the process, and making it accessible to beginners. It's like assembling a Lego set, where each piece fits into a larger picture, revealing the intricacies of AI modeling. Interactive quizzes play a crucial role, too. They test your comprehension and retention, offering instant feedback that reinforces learning. These quizzes are not just about right or wrong answers; they're about understanding your strengths and areas for improvement. By actively engaging with the material, you cement your knowledge, making it second nature.

For those eager to dive into interactive learning, several platforms stand out as excellent resources. Codecademy offers an interactive coding environment that guides you through exercises step by step, providing hands-on experience in a supportive setting. It's like having a personal tutor who's always ready to help you tackle new challenges. DataCamp provides hands-on data science projects, allowing you to apply AI concepts in practical, real-world scenarios. These projects are designed to deepen your understanding and develop your skills, turning theory into practice. By incorporating these platforms into your learning regimen, you open up a world of possibilities where learning becomes an adventure, not a chore.

Interactive learning is not just a method; it's an experience that changes how you perceive AI. It bridges the gap between knowing and doing, allowing you to explore, experiment, and ultimately excel. Whether you're debugging code, optimizing algorithms, or simply exploring new ideas, these exercises equip you with the tools you need to succeed. So, get ready to roll up your sleeves and dive into the world of AI, where the only limit is your curiosity.

9.2 UTILIZING INFOGRAPHICS FOR AI COMPREHENSION

Imagine trying to explain AI with just words, like describing a color to someone who's never seen it. That's why infographics are such a game-changer. They're like the Swiss army knife of information, distilling complex AI data into something you can glance at and get immediately. They shine when summarizing AI trends and statistics, allowing you to grasp the big picture without getting lost in the weeds. Visual comparisons of AI models and techniques can show you at a glance how different approaches stack up against each other, making them invaluable for anyone trying to understand the nuances of AI technologies. It's like having a cheat sheet that doesn't just help you pass the test but actually makes you excited to learn more.

Creating compelling infographics is both a science and an art. It's about striking just the right balance between text and visuals, ensuring neither overwhelms the other. Think of it like making a pizza—too much cheese, and you can't taste the sauce; too little, and it feels like you're eating cardboard. Infographics should be clear, concise, and visually engaging. Use icons and symbols to represent data points; they're the emojis of the data world, conveying complex ideas with just a glance. This approach not only enhances retention but also makes the information more relatable. After all, a well-placed icon can communicate more than a paragraph of text ever could. It's about telling a story, one that captivates and educates without sending your audience into a snooze-fest.

A well-crafted infographic is worth a thousand words or at least a few hundred PowerPoint slides. Take, for instance, infographic timelines of AI development milestones. They offer a visual journey through the history of AI, highlighting key break-throughs and moments of innovation. You get to see how far we've come and where we're headed, all laid out in a visually appealing format that encourages exploration. Visual explainer guides on AI ethics and implications, on the other hand, tackle the more complex and often abstract aspects of AI, making them accessible to everyone. These infographics simplify ethical dilemmas and societal impacts, opening up discussions that might otherwise be too daunting. They're like a good movie trailer— giving you just enough to get hooked without spoiling the story.

If you're eager to dive into infographic design, there are tools out there that make the process as easy as pie. Piktochart is fantastic for those new to the game, offering user-friendly creation that doesn't require a design degree to navigate. It's like having a graphic designer in your back pocket, ready to whip up some-thing impressive at a moment's notice. Venngage is another excel-lent option, providing customizable templates that allow you to tailor your infographics to suit your needs. Whether you're creating content for a presentation, a blog post, or a social media campaign, these tools can help you craft infographics that not only convey your message but do so with style and flair.

Interactive Element: Infographic Design Challenge

Try your hand at creating an infographic that explains a simple AI concept, like how neural networks function. Use tools like Piktochart or Venngage to design your infographic, focusing on balancing visuals and text for maximum impact. Share your creation with peers for feedback and see how different approaches can enhance understanding.

9.3 INCORPORATING AI IN CREATIVE PROJECTS

Picture yourself as an artist with a blank canvas, a world of possibilities stretching before you. Now imagine AI as your trusty paintbrush, ready to bring your wildest visions to life. AI's role in creativity is like adding a splash of magic to your toolkit. It doesn't replace your unique flair; instead, it elevates it, offering new avenues for expression you might not have considered. Take AI-generated visual art, for instance—think of it as having a digital assistant that conjures up stunning visuals based on your input. Whether it's crafting surreal landscapes or abstract portraits, AI can create imagery that pushes the boundaries of traditional art. Animations, too, benefit from AI's touch, with algorithms capable of generating fluid, lifelike movements that would take ages by hand. It's akin to having a team of animators at your fingertips, ready to bring your stories to life with breathtaking detail.

Let's talk about writing. Imagine you're staring at a blank page, the cursor blinking like a persistent butler asking for your command. Enter AI, your literary accomplice, ready to turn your fleeting thoughts into prose. With AI assistance, you can jump-start your creative writing by generating ideas, drafting outlines, or even crafting entire paragraphs. It's like having a brain-storming partner who never tires, always ready with a suggestion or a plot twist. AI doesn't write your story for you, but it sure gets the creative juices flowing, helping you overcome writer's block and explore narrative paths you might not have considered.

Music and sound design are no strangers to the AI revolution either. Imagine composing a symphony with an AI collaborator who understands harmony and rhythm, as well as any seasoned composer. AI tools can help you create music that resonates, whether you're scoring a film or crafting a catchy jingle. It's like having a digital orchestra at your command, ready to play the melodies that exist only in your mind. In video editing, AI can optimize footage, suggesting cuts and effects that enhance the narrative without overshadowing your vision. It's akin to having a seasoned editor who knows exactly what your project needs to shine.

Examples of AI in creative fields are as diverse as they are inspiring. Take AI-assisted photography, where algorithms enhance images with precision, adjusting lighting and color balance and even removing unwanted objects with a click. It's like having a professional retoucher on standby, ensuring your photos capture the perfect moment. In digital storytelling, AI-generated narratives allow creators to explore new dimensions in storytelling, crafting tales that engage and surprise. Imagine a story that evolves based on reader interactions, each decision shaping the narrative in unique ways.

The beauty of AI in creativity lies in its invitation to experiment and explore. It encourages you to step outside your comfort zone and to try new techniques and styles. Collaborative AI-human art initiatives are popping up everywhere, blending the best of both worlds to create art that challenges and delights. These projects showcase the potential for AI to inspire and innovate, pushing artists to explore realms they might never have ventured into alone. Interactive installations using AI technology invite audiences to engage and become part of the art itself. Imagine walking into a room where your presence influences the visuals and sounds, creating a living, breathing artwork that reacts to its environment.

As you consider incorporating AI into your creative projects, embrace the potential for innovation. Allow AI to enhance your unique voice, to complement your skills, and expand your horizons. Whether you're a painter, writer, musician, or filmmaker, AI offers tools that can inspire and elevate your work. It's about finding that perfect balance, where technology and creativity dance together, creating something truly extraordinary.

CHAPTER 10

THE FUTURE OF AI

Picture this: you're in a world where your refrigerator not only tells you what's running low but also predicts when you'll crave that midnight snack. This is not just the stuff of sci-fi dreams but an emerging reality, thanks to the mind-boggling advancements in AI technology. As we stand at the threshold of this brave new world, it's worth peeking into the crystal ball to see what's coming our way. From quantum leaps in computing to AI's cosmic aspirations, the future is a playground of possibilities.

The next big thing to watch out for is quantum computing, a technological marvel that redefines what's possible. Unlike classical computers that use bits (the digital equivalent of on/off switches), quantum computers use qubits, which can exist in multiple states at once. This means they can process information a gazillion times faster than your trusty old laptop. Imagine solving complex problems in seconds that would take traditional computers millennia to crack. Quantum Artificial Intelligence (QAI) is set to revolutionize fields like pharmaceutical development, cybersecurity, and even weather forecasting, transforming AI's capabilities to new heights. With companies like IBM and

Google leading the charge, we're inching closer to a world where QAI becomes commonplace, opening doors to futuristic applications we can only begin to imagine.

But that's not all. Enter neuromorphic computing, the tech world's latest brainchild. Inspired by the human brain's structure and function, neuromorphic chips are designed to process information in a way that's more akin to our gray matter. This allows for more efficient, energy-saving computations, potentially revolutionizing everything from autonomous vehicles to personal gadgets. It's like giving AI its own set of neurons, allowing it to think and react more naturally. As we continue to blur the lines between human intelligence and machine learning, the potential for these technologies to reshape industries and redefine what's possible is staggering.

AI is not just sticking to its usual haunts; it's boldly venturing into new domains, like space exploration and personalized medicine. In the vast expanses of space, AI is helping astronomers make sense of the cosmos, analyzing data from telescopes to identify celestial phenomena faster than any human could. It's like having a cosmic tour guide pointing out every twinkling wonder in the night sky. Meanwhile, down here on Earth, AI is making waves in personalized medicine. By analyzing genetic information, AI can tailor treatments to individual patients, ensuring that medicine is as unique as your fingerprint. This isn't just a leap forward; it's a giant leap for mankind, promising a future where healthcare is more precise and personal than ever before.

AI's impact isn't limited to the stars or the hospital ward; it's also taking on global challenges like climate change and food security. In the battle against climate change, AI models predict climate patterns, helping scientists develop strategies to mitigate the impact of global warming. Picture AI as Mother Nature's assistant, meticulously analyzing data to protect our planet. In agriculture, AI-driven innovations are making farming more sustainable, optimizing resources to ensure that every seed counts. From predicting crop yields to managing water usage, AI is turning farmers into tech-savvy stewards of the land, ensuring that the world's growing population doesn't go hungry.

As we look to the future, the possibilities for AI seem as limitless as the universe itself. Imagine AI in autonomous urban planning, designing cities that are smarter, greener, and more efficient. Or consider AI's integration with augmented and virtual reality, creating immersive experiences that blur the lines between digital and physical worlds. It's like stepping into a video game where the world adapts to your every move, offering experiences that are as personalized as they are awe-inspiring.

Reflection Section: Envisioning AI's Future

Take a moment to envision how AI could transform an area of your life or work. What futuristic applications can you imagine? Jot down your ideas and consider how they might align with emerging AI trends. This exercise encourages creative thinking and can inspire new perspectives on how AI might shape the future you envision.

10.1 PREPARING FOR AI'S FUTURE: SKILLS TO DEVELOP

As the AI landscape rapidly evolves, preparing yourself with the right skills is akin to stocking a toolbox with essentials for an unpredictable journey. First on the list is mastering programming languages like Python and R. These aren't just for developers anymore; they're becoming the lingua franca of data-driven decision-making. Whether you're automating mundane tasks or designing complex algorithms, a solid grasp of these languages can open doors to a myriad of opportunities. Think of them as your trusty Swiss Army knife, versatile and indispensable. But don't stop there. Cultivate strong analytical and critical thinking abilities. AI thrives on data—lots of it—and your ability to sift through this deluge, spotting patterns and making informed decisions, will set you apart. It's like being a detective in a sea of numbers, piecing together clues to solve the grand puzzle.

Yet, in this AI-empowered world, technical prowess alone won't suffice. Interdisciplinary knowledge is your secret weapon. By blending AI expertise with insights from other fields, you can spark innovation and foster new perspectives. Consider the burgeoning field of AI applications in law and ethics. As AI systems become more embedded in daily life, navigating the legal and ethical implications becomes crucial. Picture AI algorithms in courtrooms, aiding in legal decision-making, or in hospitals, ensuring patient privacy. The cross-pollination of AI with disciplines like law or humanities can lead to groundbreaking advancements. Furthermore, collaborative research across fields often results in novel solutions that wouldn't emerge in isolation. It's like a jam session where each musician brings their unique sound, creating a symphony that's richer and more complex.

Creative problem-solving is another skill you can't afford to overlook. AI, with all its power, still requires a human touch to guide it effectively. Design thinking approaches can help you tackle AI projects with a user-centric focus, ensuring that technology serves real needs rather than just being flashy. Consider scenario planning, a technique that allows you to anticipate various future possibilities and devise strategies accordingly. It's like playing chess with the future, considering each move and its potential outcomes. By honing these skills, you'll be better equipped to leverage AI technologies in ways that are innovative and effective.

In this ever-fluctuating world, emotional intelligence and adaptability are your anchors. As AI continues to reshape industries, the ability to build collaborative team dynamics becomes invaluable. AI may handle data, but humans handle emotions and relationships. Your ability to manage change and uncertainty—skills that AI cannot replicate—will help you navigate AI-driven environments. Think of it as being the calm captain of a ship navigating stormy seas. Your adaptability allows you to adjust sails, ensuring smooth sailing even in turbulent waters. Emotional intelligence ensures you remain connected to your crew, fostering a supportive and cohesive team atmosphere.

These skills are not just about staying relevant; they are about thriving in a world increasingly intertwined with AI. Embrace the change, arm yourself with these capabilities, and you'll find that the future, while uncertain, is full of potential.

10.2 ADAPTING TO AI INNOVATIONS IN THE WORKPLACE

Step into any bustling office today, and you might notice that AI is quietly reshaping the way we work. It's like having a diligent assistant who never takes a coffee break. For many, this means a shift in job roles and responsibilities. Take administrative positions, for example. Once filled with repetitive tasks like data entry and scheduling, these roles are being transformed by automation. AI handles the mundane, freeing up human talent for more engaging work. This change is akin to having a self-driving car—you're still in control, but the heavy lifting is done for you. As AI takes over the chores, employees are finding their skill sets evolving, with an increased emphasis on strategic thinking and problem-solving.

In management, AI is becoming a decision-making ally. Picture it as a savvy consultant who processes data faster than you can say "spreadsheet." AI tools analyze vast amounts of information, providing insights that help managers make informed decisions. It's not about AI taking over but enhancing human capabilities, much like a trusted adviser whispering in your ear. With AI, managers can focus on strategy and leadership, leaving the number crunching to algorithms. This shift means that leadership roles are also evolving, demanding a blend of technical know-how and people skills. As AI continues to integrate into workplaces, adapting to these changes becomes not just necessary but beneficial.

So, how do we prepare ourselves and our teams for this AI-driven world? Upskilling and reskilling are the buzzwords of the day. Employees need opportunities to learn and grow, adapting their skills to meet the demands of a changing landscape. Offering training in AI tools and technologies is a start. Think of it as equipping your team with a new set of tools for the digital age. But it's not just about technology. Encouraging soft skills like communication and teamwork is equally important. By integrating AI into daily workflows, you create a seamless blend of human and machine, where each complements the other. This symbiosis leads to increased productivity and innovation, setting the stage for continued success.

AI also plays a significant role in enhancing collaboration. With AI-driven platforms, team communication reaches new heights. Imagine a digital workspace where ideas flow freely and collaboration happens in real time, regardless of location. AI tools facilitate this by offering real-time translation and communication aids. It's like having a universal translator in your pocket, breaking down language barriers and fostering understanding. These tools not only enhance communication but also promote a more cohesive work environment. Teams become more agile, adapting quickly to changes and challenges. AI doesn't replace human interaction but enriches it, allowing for creativity and innovation to thrive.

Creating a culture of innovation and learning is crucial in this AI-centric environment. Encourage your team to experiment with AI solutions. Think of it as a sandbox for creativity, where ideas are nurtured and explored without fear of failure. This mindset fosters continuous learning, as employees are encouraged to embrace new challenges and opportunities. Providing learning opportunities for AI skill development not only enhances individual growth but also benefits the organization as a whole. It's like planting seeds in a garden, where each new skill and idea contributes to a flourishing ecosystem. As AI continues to evolve, remaining curious and open to learning ensures that you and your team stay competitive and relevant.

10.3 LIFELONG LEARNING IN THE AI ERA

Picture this: AI is changing faster than you can say "neural network," and keeping up with it feels like running a never-ending marathon. But here's the twist—this marathon is one where you can actually enjoy the journey because it's not about speed but about continuous improvement. Lifelong learning isn't just a trendy buzzword; it's your golden ticket to staying relevant in an ever-evolving world. Embracing this mindset means you're always on the lookout for new skills, like a curious explorer charting uncharted territories. Staying informed about the latest AI research isn't just for techies; it's for anyone who wants to keep their finger on the pulse of what's next. Think of it as reading the morning paper over your coffee, only with a dash of future.

Now, let's talk about how to keep learning without burning out. The beauty of today's educational landscape is that it's as flexible as a yoga instructor. Online courses and certifications offer a treasure trove of knowledge at your fingertips. Whether you're a night owl or an early bird, there's a class to fit your schedule. Workshops and webinars are like mini-adventures into emerging AI topics, giving you a taste of what's fresh without a long-term commitment. These bite-sized learning opportunities allow you to dip your toes into new areas, expanding your skill set at your own pace. It's like customizing your education to fit your lifestyle, turning learning into a hobby rather than a chore.

AI is also stepping up as a personal tutor, making learning more personalized than ever. With AI-powered adaptive learning platforms, you get a tailor-made educational experience that caters to your individual needs. These platforms analyze your progress and adjust content accordingly, ensuring you're constantly challenged but never overwhelmed. It's like having a personal trainer for your brain, pushing you just enough to keep you growing. Personalized content recommendations further enhance this experience, guiding you to resources that align with your interests and skill level. This isn't just about acing a course; it's about fostering a genuine love for learning that keeps you engaged and motivated.

But learning isn't just a solitary endeavor. Networking and knowledge sharing are vital components of professional growth, and here's where AI-focused conferences and meetups come into play. These events are more than just opportunities to collect business cards; they're spaces where ideas flourish and collaborations are born. Engaging in collaborative research and projects allows you to share insights and learn from others, creating a rich tapestry of shared knowledge. It's like being part of a think tank where every voice contributes to a bigger picture. By building these networks, you open doors to opportunities that might otherwise remain hidden, enriching your learning experience and professional journey.

In this AI-driven era, learning is a lifelong pursuit. It's not about reaching a destination but about continuously evolving and adapting to new challenges. Whether through flexible learning opportunities or personalized experiences, the path to growth is paved with curiosity and collaboration. As you navigate this landscape, remember that your journey is uniquely yours, shaped by the choices you make and the connections you foster. With each step, you not only enhance your own skills but also contribute to a larger community of learners, shaping the future of AI together. So, as we turn the page to explore what's next, keep your mind open and your curiosity alive.

CHAPTER 11

INSPIRING AI SUCCESS STORIES

Imagine waking up to find your coffee brewed, your car warmed up, and your emails sorted by importance—all while you were dreaming of tropical vacations. Welcome to the world of AI, where the mundane gets a tech-savvy upgrade, and you get to focus on the big picture. Now, imagine what happens when this technology scales beyond your morning routine to disrupt entire industries. We're not just talking about incremental change; we're talking about revolutions. In this chapter, we'll meet the trailblazers who took the AI bull by the horns and transformed industries, making waves that ripple through our daily lives.

11.1 INNOVATORS WHO TRANSFORMED INDUSTRIES WITH AI

Let's start with healthcare, an industry often bogged down by paperwork and long wait times. Enter AI, the newest member of the diagnostic team, armed not with a stethoscope but with algorithms capable of analyzing medical images with laser precision. Stanford University, for instance, developed an AI system that diagnoses pneumonia from X-rays more accurately than seasoned radiologists. Talk about a second opinion! And that's just the beginning. IBM Watson, with its insatiable appetite for data, once identified a rare form of leukemia in a patient that stumped human doctors. It's like having a doctor who never sleeps, continually learning from every piece of medical literature it consumes. These tales aren't just about faster diagnoses; they're about saving lives and trimming the fat from operational costs, proving that AI is more than a buzzword—it's a game-changer.

The automotive industry, too, is experiencing its AI renaissance. Remember when self-driving cars seemed like something only James Bond would have access to? Not anymore. AI is the unsung hero behind the wheel, interpreting everything from traffic lights to unexpected jaywalkers with the swiftness of a seasoned driver. Neural networks mimic our brains, recognizing patterns and making split-second decisions. The result? Autonomous vehicles that don't just drive but anticipate, enhancing safety and efficiency on our roads. It's not just about getting from point A to B; it's about redefining the journey itself. With each mile, AI is not just changing how we travel but paving the path for more innovative, greener cities.

How did these innovators pull it off? It wasn't just about having a great idea; it was about execution, strategy, and a bit of audacity. They crafted AI-driven business models that were not just profitable but visionary. Partnerships were vital—think of them as the ultimate tag team, combining strengths to leap over regulatory hurdles and scalability issues. Navigating regulations in AI can feel like trying to dance through a minefield. Yet, these pioneers managed to waltz through with finesse, working closely with governments and regulatory bodies to ensure compliance while pushing the envelope of what's possible. Scalability, another hurdle, was tackled by investing in robust AI infrastructures that could grow alongside their ambitions. It was no small feat, but these visionaries made it happen, one calculated risk at a time.

So, what's the takeaway for those of you considering an AI endeavor? First and foremost, adaptability is your best friend. The AI landscape is as dynamic as a stock market on caffeine, and staying nimble is crucial. Resilience, too, is critical—because, let's face it, setbacks are inevitable. But remember, each hurdle is just an opportunity to learn and innovate. Finally, never lose sight of the customer. A customer-centric approach in AI applications ensures that your solutions are not just technically sound but genuinely valuable. It's about creating AI that not only works but truly serves, enhancing the human experience rather than complicating it.

11.2 PERSONAL GROWTH THROUGH AI: INSPIRING JOURNEYS

Picture this: a seasoned accountant named Sarah, armed with her trusty calculator, suddenly finds herself in the brave new world of AI. Initially hesitant, she decides to embrace the change and transitions into a data analyst role, a move that feels like leaping off a cliff with a parachute she barely knows how to operate. But Sarah is not alone. Many individuals have pivoted from traditional roles to AI-centric careers, driven by the promise of innovation and opportunity. These transitions are not just about learning new skills; they're about redefining one's professional identity in a world that's evolving faster than you can say "machine learning." Sarah's story mirrors many others who have leveraged AI as a stepping stone to entrepreneurial success, launching startups that capitalize on AI's ability to solve complex problems with the precision of a Swiss watch.

Now, let's talk about skill development. AI isn't just a tool; it's a catalyst for growth, pushing individuals to acquire competencies that were once the domain of computer scientists. Take John, a graphic designer who once thought neural networks were something for tech geeks. He discovered AI's potential to enhance his creative skills, using AI-powered tools to generate stunning visuals that leave his clients in awe. By diving into AI-focused education and training, John didn't just upskill—he transformed. His journey highlights how AI can empower you to think outside the box, whether you're crafting a digital masterpiece or analyzing data trends with the understanding of a seasoned analyst. The beauty of AI is its versatility, offering a buffet of skills that cater to both creative and analytical minds.

Of course, every silver lining has its cloud. Balancing AI learning with life's other commitments can feel like juggling flaming torches while riding a unicycle. But here's the kicker: AI can also be the key to overcoming these challenges. Consider Emma, a busy mother of two who managed to squeeze AI courses into her packed schedule. Her secret? AI-driven learning platforms offering flexible, personalized education that fits around school runs and bedtime stories. Emma's journey underscores the importance of building confidence with AI technologies, transforming them from intimidating specters into friendly allies. For those feeling daunted by the prospect of diving into AI, remember that the first step is often the hardest. Once you overcome that initial hurdle, you might find yourself wondering why you didn't start sooner.

Practical advice for anyone looking to integrate AI into their personal growth journey? Start with clear, achievable goals. Think of your AI learning path as a road trip, with milestones that keep you motivated and destination points that mark your progress. Set realistic expectations—you won't become an AI guru overnight, but each small step is progress. Be proactive in your learning. Dive into resources, experiment with tools, and don't be afraid to make mistakes. After all, failures are just stepping stones to success, each one teaching you something new about AI and your own capabilities. Embrace a mindset of curiosity and resilience because the landscape of AI is always shifting, offering new opportunities and challenges that can propel your growth in unexpected ways.

11.3 AI IN EDUCATION: TRANSFORMING LEARNING LANDSCAPES

Imagine your school days juggling textbooks, teachers, and timetables. Now, picture an educational environment where AI acts as your personal tutor, guiding you through lessons tailored just for you. AI is reshaping traditional education models by introducing adaptive learning platforms that cater to individual needs. These platforms are like having a teacher who knows exactly which topics you struggle with and adjusts the lesson plan accordingly. Whether you're a math whiz or a history buff, AI ensures that your learning path is as unique as your fingerprint. It's a bit like having a gym trainer who knows your strengths and pushes you just enough to keep you improving without breaking a sweat—or a leg.

Innovative educational initiatives have embraced AI with open arms, integrating it in creative ways that would make even the most stoic headmaster crack a smile. In STEM education, AI is the catalyst that transforms abstract concepts into interactive experiences. Imagine using virtual labs where you can experiment, fail, and try again without the fear of blowing up the chemistry lab. AI-driven content creation is another marvel, allowing educators to generate rich, engaging materials that capture the imagination. With AI, a dusty history lesson morphs into an interactive timeline, bringing characters and events to life right before your eyes. It's education that feels less like a chore and more like a choose-your-own-adventure novel.

The benefits AI brings to both students and educators are substantial and, frankly, quite exciting. For students, AI removes barriers to quality education. No longer are top-notch resources confined to elite institutions; AI democratizes access, offering personalized learning experiences to anyone with an internet connection. It's the difference between a one-size-fits-all sweater and a custom-tailored suit. For educators, AI tools streamline administrative tasks, freeing up time to focus on teaching rather than paperwork. Imagine a world where grading is automated, lesson plans are generated in seconds, and classroom management is as simple as tapping an app. Teachers can dedicate more time to what they do best: inspiring and nurturing young minds.

Looking ahead, the future of AI in education is filled with possibilities that could redefine learning as we know it. Lifelong learning becomes not just a buzzword but a reality, with AI facilitating professional development and skill acquisition well into adulthood. Imagine AI as your lifelong partner, helping you navigate career transitions and personal growth with ease. On a global scale, AI holds the promise of bridging educational gaps and bringing quality learning experiences to underserved regions. It's a vision of a world where education knows no borders, where a child in a remote village has the same access to learning as one in a bustling city. This democratization of education could become one of AI's most profound impacts.

Interactive Element: AI Education Reflection

Consider how AI has influenced your own learning experiences, whether through online courses, educational apps, or other resources. Reflect on how these tools have impacted your approach to learning and identify any areas where AI could further enhance your educational journey. Write down your thoughts and ideas, envisioning how AI might play a role in your future learning endeavors.

AI's impact on education is not just about technology; it's about transforming how we learn, teach, and grow. It's about creating opportunities that were once unimaginable, making learning an engaging, personalized, and accessible experience for all. Whether you're a student eager to explore new subjects or an educator looking to innovate, AI offers a toolkit that can enrich every aspect of education.

11.4 FROM IDEA TO REALITY: AI-DRIVEN ACHIEVEMENTS

Imagine AI stepping into the ring to tackle environmental challenges. It's not just a digital superhero; it's a game-changer in conservation. AI applications in environmental conservation are turning conceptual dreams into impactful realities. Picture drones equipped with AI that can scan vast forest areas, identifying illegal logging activities with the precision of an eagle's eye. This technology saves countless trees by alerting authorities before significant damage occurs, like a high-tech forest ranger. Moreover, AI assists in monitoring endangered species. It analyzes data from camera traps and sound sensors, helping conservationists track animal movements and behaviors with unprecedented accuracy. This isn't just about protecting wildlife; it's about preserving the delicate balance of our ecosystems.

Urban planning is another area where AI rolls up its sleeves and gets to work. Smart cities aren't just futuristic fantasies; they're becoming reality with AI-driven solutions. Consider traffic management systems that use AI to optimize traffic flow, reducing congestion and emissions. These systems analyze real-time data from cameras and sensors, adjusting traffic lights and public transport schedules on the fly. It's like having a city planner who never sleeps, always finding ways to make commutes smoother and cities greener. AI also plays a role in energy management, predicting demand and optimizing resource distribution, ensuring the city runs efficiently while reducing its carbon footprint. These transformations make urban areas not only more livable but also more sustainable.

Turning AI ideas into tangible projects requires a mix of creativity and strategy. Prototyping and testing are crucial stages, akin to rehearsing a play before opening night. Developers create initial versions of their AI solutions and test them rigorously, ironing out glitches and refining functionalities. It's an iterative process, demanding patience and precision—think of it as crafting a delicate soufflé, where every ingredient must be perfectly measured. Securing funding and resources is another critical step. AI initiatives often require significant investment, which means pitching ideas to investors and stakeholders who can provide the necessary support. It's a bit like Shark Tank, with innovators presenting their visions to those who hold the purse strings, convincing them of the potential impact and return on investment.

Collaborations and partnerships are the secret sauce behind many successful AI projects. Cross-disciplinary collaborations bring together experts from various fields, each contributing unique insights and skills. Imagine a team of ecologists, data scientists, and AI engineers working together to create a conservation tool that not only tracks wildlife but also predicts poaching hotspots. These collaborations are the epitome of synergy, where the sum is greater than its parts. Partnerships between academia and industry also play a pivotal role. Universities often drive research and innovation, while industries provide the practical applications and scalability. This partnership creates a pipeline from research labs to real-world solutions, ensuring that AI innovations are not only groundbreaking but also impactful.

For those of you dreaming of turning your AI ideas into reality, take heart from the stories of these trailblazers. Experimentation and risk-taking are crucial. Don't be afraid to try new approaches or pivot when things don't go as planned. Remember that failure is often a stepping stone to success, offering invaluable lessons along the way. Perseverance is equally important, and the journey from concept to reality can be long and challenging, but vision and determination will keep you moving forward. Keep your eyes on the prize, and remember that innovation often comes from those willing to push boundaries and think outside the box. As you navigate this path, draw inspiration from those who have walked it before, and let their achievements fuel your ambition.

As you reflect on these AI success stories, remember that each innovation began as a simple idea. With dedication and collaboration, your own AI projects can transform from concepts to reality, impacting industries and lives.

CHAPTER 12

BUILDING YOUR AI JOURNEY

Picture this: you're standing at the foot of a mountain with a backpack full of potential and only a vague idea of what's at the summit. Welcome to the world of AI—an exhilarating climb filled with opportunities to learn, grow, and conquer. But before you start sprinting up that steep trail, let's talk about setting some goals. You see, without a clear destination, even the most enthusiastic climber can end up wandering in circles. This is where the magic of goal setting comes into play—not just any goals, but the kind that transforms lofty dreams into achievable milestones.

Having clear goals is like having a GPS for your AI journey. It provides direction and motivation, keeping you focused on what matters most. Whether you're an entrepreneur eyeing AI to boost your business, a designer looking to innovate, or a student diving into new tech, aligning your AI goals with both personal and professional aspirations is crucial. Imagine long-term visions of mastering AI skills like a seasoned chef perfecting a signature dish, blending knowledge, creativity, and a dash of persistence.

These goals aren't just about reaching an endpoint but about enriching your journey with purpose and passion.

Crafting SMART goals—Specific, Measurable, Achievable, Relevant, and Time-bound—is your recipe for success. Picture setting a goal to complete a specific AI course within three months. This isn't just a pipe dream; it's a tangible target. Start by breaking it down: what specific knowledge do you want to gain? How will you measure your progress? Is it achievable within your current schedule? Ensure it's relevant to your broader aspirations, and set a clear timeline. Weekly assessments are like checkpoints along the way, ensuring you're on track and adjusting as needed. By applying the SMART framework, you're not just setting goals; you're creating a structured plan that transforms potential stumbling blocks into stepping stones.

Tracking your progress is crucial because, let's face it, even the best-laid plans can veer off course. Utilize AI-powered apps designed for goal tracking to keep your eyes on the prize. These digital companions can manage your milestones, providing nudges and insights to help you maintain momentum. Regular self-assessments and reflections act as your compass, guiding you through the fog and ensuring you're not just busy but productive. Embracing these tools is like having a personal coach cheering you on, celebrating your wins, and helping you learn from setbacks.

Now, let's talk about the art of reviewing and adjusting your goals. Much like a skilled sailor who frequently checks the wind and adjusts the sails, you too should revisit your goals regularly. Monthly review sessions allow you to evaluate your progress and ensure your goals still align with your evolving interests and skills. Perhaps you've developed a new passion for prompt engineering or discovered an unexpected knack for creative AI applications.

Adjusting your goals to incorporate these new interests not only keeps your journey exciting but also ensures continued growth and adaptation. Embrace this fluidity; after all, the only constant in the world of AI is change.

Interactive Element: Goal-Tracking Worksheet

Create a personalized goal-tracking worksheet using an AI-powered app or a simple spreadsheet. Outline your SMART goals, set weekly checkpoints, and include space for reflections and adjustments. Use this worksheet to document your journey, celebrate milestones, and pivot strategies when necessary. Let this be your roadmap, guiding you toward AI mastery with clarity and focus.

12.1 CULTIVATING A GROWTH MINDSET WITH AI

Imagine you're trying to grow a plant indoors. You water it, give it sunlight, and even talk to it like a best friend. Sometimes, despite your best efforts, the leaves droop. Do you give up? Of course not! You adjust, maybe move it closer to the window or change the soil. This is the essence of a growth mindset—seeing setbacks not as failures but as opportunities to learn and adapt. In the world of AI, this mindset is crucial. It's about embracing challenges and seeing every hiccup as a stepping stone to mastery. Whether you're debugging a stubborn piece of code or refining a prompt, every mistake is a lesson in disguise. Persistence is your secret weapon, turning what seems like a dead end into a detour that leads to new insights and skills.

Embracing a growth mindset is more than just an attitude; it's a practice. One way to foster this mindset is by welcoming constructive feedback. Think of feedback as your GPS, recalibrating your path to ensure you're heading in the right direction. When working on AI projects, seek out critiques from peers or mentors. They might highlight blind spots or suggest new approaches, helping you refine your work. Another strategy is to set incremental challenges. These are like mini-bosses in a video game, pushing you to level up without overwhelming you. Maybe start with a simple AI task, then gradually tackle more complex problems as your confidence grows. Each challenge conquered is a confidence boost, reinforcing your belief in your ability to learn and adapt.

The benefits of a growth mindset in AI are immense. It breeds adaptability, an invaluable trait in a field where change is the only constant. As new technologies emerge, those with a growth mindset embrace them with curiosity, eager to explore and experiment. This adaptability enhances problem-solving capabilities, allowing you to approach AI challenges with a creative and open mind. Instead of seeing a roadblock, you see a puzzle waiting to be solved, and this perspective fuels innovation. In AI, where the landscape is ever-evolving, being a flexible thinker is your best asset, turning potential disruptions into opportunities for creativity and success.

Consider Sarah, an AI enthusiast who initially struggled with machine learning algorithms. Her first attempts were far from perfect, leading to countless errors. But instead of giving up, she saw each error as a clue, a hint toward understanding the underlying patterns. She sought feedback, attended workshops, and gradually improved her skills. Today, Sarah leads a team developing innovative AI solutions, and her journey is a testament to the power of persistence and adaptability. Then there's Mike, a developer who found himself at a crossroads when his industry shifted toward AI. Rather than resist, he embraced this change, enrolling in AI courses and experimenting with new tools. His willingness to pivot and learn opened doors to opportunities he never imagined, propelling his career into exciting new territories.

Reflection Section: Growth Mindset Journal

Keep a journal to track your AI learning experiences. Note the challenges you encounter, the solutions you try, and the insights you gain. Reflect on the feedback received and how it influences your growth. Review these entries regularly to see how your mindset evolves and strengthens over time.

12.2 EMBRACING CHALLENGES AS LEARNING OPPORTUNITIES

Imagine learning AI is like tackling a giant, deliciously complicated puzzle. Each piece represents a challenge, and when you fit them together, you get the bigger picture. Challenges aren't just obstacles—they're catalysts for growth. They push you to stretch your skills and think differently. Each time you face a problem, you're building confidence, refining your techniques, and learning something new. The beauty of AI is in its complexity. It's like learning a new language, where each mistake is a lesson in vocabulary and grammar. Just like muscle gains from lifting weights, your AI skills strengthen with every problem you solve. Mistakes aren't setbacks; they're stepping stones to mastery. So when you stumble, please take a deep breath and see it as a chance to refine your approach and come back stronger.

Overcoming challenges in AI doesn't require a PhD in computer science. It's about strategy and community. Start by breaking problems into bite-sized tasks. If you're faced with a complex algorithm that feels like it's written in hieroglyphics, break it down. Tackle one part at a time. Maybe it's understanding the underlying math today and coding it tomorrow. This approach makes even the most daunting tasks manageable. And remember, you're not alone. There's a whole world of AI enthusiasts ready to help. Seek support from AI communities and mentors who've walked the path before you. They offer insights and tips that can illuminate your way through the murky waters of AI challenges. Sometimes, a fresh perspective is all you need to see the solution.

Facing challenges head-on doesn't just solve problems—it transforms you. By persevering through difficulties, you develop resilience, a trait that will serve you well beyond AI. Each challenge overcome is a badge of honor, a testament to your grit. As you solve problems, you're not just learning AI; you're learning about yourself. You're discovering your limits and pushing past them, achieving breakthroughs that once seemed impossible. Embracing challenges enhances your expertise and opens new doors. You'll find yourself more confident in your abilities, ready to tackle even the most intimidating AI projects. This growth isn't just personal; it's professional, setting you apart as someone who doesn't shy away from the tough stuff.

Consider the story of a startup that faced a mountain of technical hurdles when deploying AI solutions. At first, each glitch felt like a potential showstopper. But by breaking problems into smaller tasks, they tackled them one by one. They leaned on the AI community for support, sharing insights, and learning from others' experiences. This collaborative approach transformed their project from a daunting challenge into a series of manageable tasks. Their persistence paid off, leading to a successful deployment that revolutionized their industry.

Then there's the tale of a researcher who turned experimental failures into triumphs. Every failed test was a lesson, each mistake a clue. They embraced these setbacks, using them to refine their techniques. Over time, what seemed like endless roadblocks became stepping stones to innovative solutions. Their willingness to learn from failure led to breakthroughs that advanced their field and earned them recognition. These stories aren't just about AI; they're about the power of perseverance and the rewards of embracing challenges. They remind us that every obstacle is an opportunity in disguise, waiting to be uncovered by those bold enough to face it.

12.3 YOUR AI JOURNEY: NEXT STEPS AND BEYOND

Imagine you're standing at the edge of a vast meadow, each blade of grass representing a new opportunity in the realm of AI. How do you navigate this landscape and choose where to plant your next seeds of knowledge? Continuing your AI education is crucial, and as the field evolves, so should your skills. Consider enrolling in advanced AI courses and certifications. These programs often delve into cutting-edge technologies and methodologies, providing you with the latest insights and techniques. Whether it's an intensive boot camp or a comprehensive online course, each learning experience is a new thread in the tapestry of your AI expertise. Participating in AI workshops and seminars can also be extremely beneficial. These interactive settings allow you to engage with experts, ask questions, and gain hands-on experience with new tools and concepts. They offer a dynamic learning environment where theory meets practice—ideal for those who thrive on interaction and immediate application.

However, learning isn't confined to the classroom or virtual settings. The real magic happens when you start applying your AI knowledge in practical scenarios. Engaging in AI-related projects, whether at work or as personal ventures, allows you to experiment and innovate. Perhaps you're working on automating a repetitive task at your job or developing an AI-driven app in your spare time. Each project is a playground for your skills, offering real-world challenges and triumphs that deepen your understanding. Don't shy away from collaborating on open-source AI projects. These initiatives not only expand your portfolio but also connect you with a community of like-minded individuals. Open-source projects are where ideas flourish, and innovation thrives, providing opportunities to contribute to groundbreaking work while learning from others in the field.

Networking is the unsung hero of any professional journey, and AI is no exception. Engaging with AI communities and networks is like having a backstage pass to the industry's latest developments. Join AI meetups and online forums where you can share ideas, seek advice, and build relationships with peers and mentors. These platforms are rich with diverse perspectives and insights, offering a treasure trove of knowledge just waiting to be tapped. Attending AI conferences and networking events further expands your horizons. Not only do they provide opportunities to learn from industry leaders, but they also allow you to showcase your own expertise. The connections you make here can lead to collaborations, job opportunities, and lifelong friendships. Networking is more than exchanging business cards; it's about building a community that supports your growth and success.

Now, take a moment to imagine your future with AI. What does it look like? Envisioning your path can be a powerful motivator, guiding your decisions and actions. Set long-term career aspirations in AI, whether it's becoming a leading expert, launching your own AI startup, or contributing to societal challenges through innovative solutions. The possibilities are as vast as they are exciting. Perhaps you're inspired to develop AI tools that address climate change or create accessible AI education programs for underserved communities. Whatever your vision, let it drive your pursuit of knowledge and excellence. Your aspirations are the stars by which you navigate the ever-expanding universe of AI. Each step you take brings you closer to turning those dreams into reality, propelling you forward in this thrilling field.

As you continue on your path, remember that learning and growth are endless. AI is not a static destination but a dynamic process. Stay curious, stay engaged, and keep pushing the boundaries of what's possible. Your journey in AI is uniquely yours, filled with opportunities to learn, create, and innovate. Embrace each challenge and triumph with enthusiasm, knowing that every experience adds depth to your understanding and expertise. The world of AI is vast and ever-changing, offering endless possibilities for those willing to explore. So go forth with confidence, knowing that your path is illuminated by the knowledge, skills, and insights you've gained. Keep reaching for the stars, and let your passion for AI guide you to new heights.

CONCLUSION

Well, here we are at the end of our AI escapade, and what a journey it has been! We've ventured into the world of AI fundamentals, unraveling the mystery behind those algorithms that sound more like a sci-fi movie than real life. We've explored how AI isn't just a high-tech gadget but a trusty sidekick ready to transform industries, from healthcare to automotive, and even revolutionize your daily grind.

You've learned that AI is not just a tool but a powerful ally in your quest for personal and professional growth. Whether you're an entrepreneur, a designer, or someone just dipping their toes into the AI pool, you now know how to leverage this technology to skyrocket your creativity and efficiency. And let's not forget those nifty AI prompts. You've become a prompt whisperer, guiding AI into producing exactly what you need, whether that's crafting the perfect social media post or generating stunning visuals.

Throughout these pages, we've also tackled the biggies—monetizing AI and its ethical implications. Remember, wielding AI comes with the responsibility to use it wisely. Harness its power to boost revenue and efficiency, but always keep ethics front and center. The AI landscape is a sprawling frontier ripe for exploration, but it demands a compass of integrity to navigate it well.

Our vision together was to empower you, a daring AI novice, not only to grasp but to confidently wield AI technologies. We've equipped you with strategies to boost productivity and creativity while also opening the door to new career possibilities. AI is not just a tool; it's a partner in your journey to innovate and excel.

Let's not forget the success stories that have peppered our journey. Remember Sarah, who leapt from spreadsheets to data analytics with AI as her parachute? Or the AI-driven startups that transformed industries by daring to think differently. These stories aren't just tales of triumph but blueprints for your own potential AI ventures. Use them as motivation to see the possibilities that AI can offer in your life.

Now, it's your turn. Step into the AI arena and set those goals. Whether it's enrolling in that AI course you've been eyeing or diving into a community of fellow AI enthusiasts, make your move. Begin applying what you've learned—experiment with AI tools and explore how they can enhance your personal and professional projects.

Embrace a growth mindset, dear reader. Challenges will come, but remember, they are your stepping stones to growth. View obstacles as learning opportunities and keep that curiosity burning bright. AI is a field that rewards the resilient and the adaptable. Let your spirit of innovation guide you through, and don't shy away from the unknown.

As you continue this AI adventure, commit to lifelong learning. Stay updated on emerging trends, and never stop seeking new knowledge. The AI world evolves fast, and so should your skills.

Be a lifelong student, always on the lookout for that next big thing that AI can offer.

Before you close this book, let me express my gratitude. Thank you for taking this journey with me. You now have the tools, insights, and confidence to make AI work for you. Remember, you're not alone in this. I'm cheering you on from the sidelines, ready to support you as you explore the dynamic, ever-changing world of AI.

Here's to your AI success story—go write it!

BONUS SECTION

Before we send you off into the world of AI, I wanted to provide you with a few sample Prompts for various situations that you can utilize to make your journey into AI a little less intimidating. As we discussed earlier in the guide, you can adjust any Prompt to make it more specific to your needs, which will help AI deliver a more targeted response.

Useful Daily Life Prompts

1. "What's one small change I can make today to improve my overall well-being?"
2. "How can I better organize my daily tasks to maximize productivity?"
3. "What are some simple recipes I can try this week to eat healthier?"

Image Creation

1. "Create an image of a serene mountain landscape at sunrise."
2. "Generate a futuristic cityscape with flying cars and neon lights."
3. "Design a cozy, rustic kitchen interior with warm lighting."

Enhanced Creativity

1. "What are some unique ways to repurpose common household items for art projects?"
2. "Can you suggest a creative writing prompt to spark my imagination?"
3. "What are some unusual music genres I should explore to inspire my creative work?"

Social Media Strategy

1. "How can I increase engagement on my social media posts?"
2. "What are effective strategies for growing my audience on Instagram?"
3. "What types of content should I create to boost my brand's visibility on LinkedIn?"

Personal Finance Growth

1. "What are some practical steps I can take to start saving more money each month?"
2. "How can I diversify my investment portfolio for better returns?"

3. "What tools can help me track my expenses more efficiently?"

Business Financial Growth

1. "What strategies can I use to increase my business's profit margins?"
2. "How can I optimize my company's cash flow management?"
3. "What are some effective ways to reduce operational costs in my business?"

Team Building

1. "What activities can improve communication and collaboration within my team?"
2. "How can I foster a positive team culture in a remote work environment?"
3. "What are some effective techniques for resolving conflicts within a team?"

Increased Retail Sales

1. "What merchandising strategies can I use to boost my retail sales?"
2. "How can I improve the customer shopping experience in my store?"
3. "What are some effective promotions to attract more customers?"

Self Help

1. "What daily habits can I adopt to improve my mental health?"
2. "How can I develop a more positive mindset in challenging situations?"
3. "What are some techniques to improve my focus and concentration?"

Using AI to Earn Income

1. "What are some AI-driven freelance opportunities I can explore to generate income?"
2. "How can I utilize AI tools to create a profitable online business?"
3. "What AI-powered platforms can help me monetize my skills effectively?"

Writing A Resume

1. "What are the key elements to include in a resume for a tech industry job?"
2. "How can I use AI tools to enhance the layout and content of my resume?"
3. "What strategies should I employ to tailor my resume for different job applications?"

Market Analysis

1. "What tools can I use to conduct a comprehensive market analysis for my industry?"
2. "How do I identify key market trends and opportunities in my sector?"

3. "What are the best practices for analyzing competitors'
    strengths and weaknesses?"

Innovation and Ideation

1. "What techniques can I use to generate innovative ideas
    in a team setting?"
2. "How can I foster a culture of creativity and innovation
    in my organization?"
3. "What are some methods for evaluating the feasibility of
    new ideas?"

Sustainability and Ethics

1. "What strategies can businesses implement to improve
    their sustainability practices?"
2. "How can I ensure ethical considerations are integrated
    into my business model?"
3. "What are the benefits of adopting sustainable practices
    for a brand's reputation?"

Technology and Integration

1. "What are the key steps for successfully integrating new
    technology into existing systems?"
2. "How can I leverage technology to enhance operational
    efficiency in my business?"
3. "What are the latest tech trends that businesses should
    be aware of for future integration?"

REFERENCES

Artificial Intelligence, Explained https://www.heinz.cmu.edu/media/2023/July/artificial-intelligence-explained

The History of Artificial Intelligence: Complete AI Timeline https://www.techtarget.com/searchenterpriseai/tip/The-history-of-artificial-intelligence-Complete-AI-timeline

What Is ChatGPT? Everything You Need to Know https://www.techtarget.com/whatis/definition/ChatGPT

Exploring Dalle-3 AI Image Generation for Book Art and ... https://www.colemanediting.co.uk/articles/beyond-traditional-design--exploring-dalle-3-ai-image-generation-for-book-art-and-covers

Generative AI: How it can be applied to business ... https://www.redhat.com/en/blog/generative-ai-business-applications

The Top AI Tools For Content Creators In 2024 https://www.forbes.com/sites/ianshepherd/2024/03/27/the-top-ai-tools-for-content-creators-in-2024/

AI-Driven Success: Social Media Strategies and Marketing ... https://www.thesocialmediahat.com/blog/ai-driven-success-social-media-strategies-and-marketing-innovations/

185 real-world gen AI use cases from the world's leading ... https://cloud.google.com/transform/101-real-world-generative-ai-use-cases-from-industry-leaders

An In-Depth Guide on AI Prompt Engineering for Beginners https://www.human-i-t.org/beginner-guide-prompt-engineering/?srsltid=AfmBOoqlQ_kZDpYuSE7nH7LSBqvw8FUN2tt0WlhgO3j7hPTBbNLcTudu

The Making of ChatGPT: From Data to Dialogue https://sitn.hms.harvard.edu/flash/2023/the-making-of-chatgpt-from-data-to-dialogue/

DALL-E Prompt Writing: How To Create Great Prompts https://foundationinc.co/lab/dall-e-prompts/

5 Common Generative AI Prompt Writing Mistakes (And ... https://www.forbes.com/sites/bernardmarr/2024/10/01/5-common-generative-ai-prompt-writing-mistakes-and-how-to-fix-them/

How to use AI to make money right now, say experts https://www.cnbc.com/2023/07/10/how-to-use-ai-to-make-money-right-now-say-experts.html

The 34 most promising AI startups of 2023, according to top ... https://www.businessinsider.com/the-most-promising-artificial-intelligence-startups-of-2023-2023-8

AI as a service (AIaaS): A beginner's guide for 2024 https://www.zendesk.com/blog/ai-as-a-service/

11 ChatGPT and Other AI Side Hustles to Boost Your Income https://www.businessin sider.com/list-6-generative-ai-side-hustles-to-boost-your-income-2023-2

Ethics guidelines for trustworthy AI https://digital-strategy.ec.europa.eu/en/library/ethics-guidelines-trustworthy-ai

AI Bias Examples https://www.ibm.com/think/topics/shedding-light-on-ai-bias-with-real-world-examples

Artificial Intelligence, Ethics, and Social Responsibility https://pecb.com/article/artifi cial-intelligence-ethics-and-social-responsibility

AI Act | Shaping Europe's digital future - European Union https://digital-strategy.ec.europa.eu/en/policies/regulatory-framework-ai

23 AI Productivity Tools to Revolutionize Your Workflow https://www.digitalocean.com/resources/articles/ai-productivity-tools

10 Best AI Project Management Software for 2024 https://www.forecast.app/blog/10-best-ai-project-management-software-you-need-for-2024

Unlocking Business Potential with Predictive Analytics https://online.mason.wm.edu/blog/predictive-analytics-in-business

AI Workflow Automation: A Powerful Step-by-Step Guide https://www.usemotion.com/blog/ai-workflow-automation

AI Simplified: A Beginner's Guide https://www.entopy.com/ai-simplified-a-beginners-guide/

How AI Is Personalizing Education For Every Student https://elearningindustry.com/how-ai-is-personalizing-education-for-every-student

Maximize Your Time Management: 4 Tips Using AI Tools ... https://www.forbes.com/sites/lucianapaulise/2024/10/22/maximize-your-time-management-4-tips-using-ai-tools-and-automation/

Top AI Communities in 2024 | AI Communities and Forums ... https://medium.com/@ davidrushford/top-ai-communities-in-2024-ai-communities-and-forums-for-machine-learning-artificial-d723352e3df4

40+ Mind-Blowing AI Tools to Know in 2024 https://niftypm.com/blog/ai-tools/

A free online introduction to artificial intelligence for non-experts https://www.elementsofai.com/

10 open source AI platforms for innovation https://www.digitalocean.com/resources/articles/open-source-ai-platforms

29+ AI Communities and Forums for Machine Learning ... https://aiuniverseexplorer.com/ai-communities/

Top 8 diagramming tools for software architecture - IcePanel https://icepanel.medium.com/top-8-diagramming-tools-for-software-architecture-2fc61d095b93

Top 10 AI-Powered Learning Platforms to Consider Today https://360learning.com/blog/ai-learning-platforms/

60 Best Infographic Examples for Beginners - Adobe https://www.adobe.com/express/discover/examples/infographic

How AI Generative Models Are Transforming Creativity https://www.forbes.com/coun

cils/forbestechcouncil/2024/10/22/how-ai-generative-models-are-transform
ing-creativity-real-world-case-studies-in-art-music-and-writing/

Quantum Artificial Intelligence Is Closer Than You Think https://www.forbes.com/sites/
jonathanreichental/2023/11/20/quantum-artificial-intelligence-is-closer-
than-you-think/

Artificial intelligence (AI) in personalized medicine https://journals.lww.com/annals-of-
medicine-and-surgery/fulltext/2023/11000/artificial_intelli
gence__ai__in_personalized.94.aspx

The Essential AI-Ready Skills Everyone Needs For ... https://www.forbes.com/sites/
bernardmarr/2024/07/29/the-essential-ai-ready-skills-everyone-needs-for-
tomorrows-jobs/

AI-Powered Collaboration: Transforming Ideation into ... https://medium.com/@xtn13/
ai-powered-collaboration-transforming-ideation-into-implementation-with-
smart-tools-86b754df322a

AI in Healthcare: Real-World Success Stories and Case ... https://www.linkedin.com/
pulse/ai-healthcare-real-world-success-stories-case-studies-avinash-chander-
m9tic

Artificial Intelligence in Autonomous Vehicles - Imagination https://www.imaginationtech.
com/future-of-automotive/how-do-autonomous-cars-work/artificial-intelli
gence-in-autonomous-vehicles/

The Power of AI in Personal Development https://www.linkedin.com/pulse/power-ai-
personal-development-waleed-a-hamada

AI Will Transform Teaching and Learning. Let's Get it Right. https://hai.stanford.edu/
news/ai-will-transform-teaching-and-learning-lets-get-it-right

How to Incorporate AI into SMART Goal Frameworks for ... https://pedagog.ai/how-to-
incorporate-ai-into-smart-goal-frameworks-for-students/

A Growth Mindset is Key to Generative AI Expertise. https://aquenttalent.com/blog/a-
growth-mindset-is-key-to-generative-ai-expertise

AI Adoption Challenges: Overcoming Hurdles for Success https://svitla.com/blog/ai-adop
tion-challenges/

Global AI Community - Connecting AI Communities around ... https://globalai.commu
nity/